POETRY FROM THE RUSSIAN UNDERGROUND

Translated and edited by JOSEPH LANGLAND,

TAMAS ACZEL, and LASZLO TIKOS

1817

POETRY FROM THE RUSSIAN UNDERGROUND

891.
7144
POETRY

A Bilingual Anthology

HARPER & ROW, PUBLISHERS

New York, Evanston, San Francisco, London

Grateful acknowledgment is made to the following for permission to reprint poems that originally appeared in Russian in their pages: *Grani, Possev, Phoenix, Sintaxis, Sfinxy,* Chekhov Publishing Corporation, *Po Sovyetskomu Soyuzu* (KRS), *Proza i Poeziya, Russkoye Slovo, Chu.*

"Drowning," "Idyll," "Conditions," and "After the War" originally appeared in English in the Spring 1968 issue of *Northwest Review.*

FIRST EDITION

Designed by Sidney Feinberg

Library of Congress Cataloging in Publication Data
Main entry under title:

Poetry from the Russian underground.
    1. Russian poetry—20th century. 2. Underground literature—Russia. 3. Russian poetry—20th century—Translations into English. 4. English poetry—Translations from Russian. I. Langland, Joseph, tr. II. Aczel, Tamas, tr. III. Tikos, Laszlo, tr.
PG3233.P55   891.7'1'4408   74-138746
ISBN 0-06-012501-2

Contents

Introduction: Notes from Underground		1
ANONYMOUS		
Etáp		20
Concentration Camp Song		24
Dubrovlag		28
BELLA AKHMADULINA		
Conjuration		30
I Swear		32
Bartholomew Night		38
PAVEL ANTAKOLSKY		
The Stalin Prize		44
ALEXANDER ARONOV		
A Little Geography		46
VLADIMIR BATSHEV		
Voices		50
Now the State Needs Me		52
Sonnet to Pasternak		54
Sonnet to L. K.		56
Variations on a Theme of Joseph Brodsky		58
Sonnet to G——ov		62
Pushkin at the Senate Square		66
Yelabuga		72
DMITRY BOBYSHEV		
Upon the Launching of a Sputnik		74
A House Was There		78

Содержание

Аноним
"Мы шли этапом"*   21
"Мне вспомнился Ванина порт"   25
Дубровлаг   29
Белла Ахмадулина
Заклинание   31
Клянусь   33
Варфоломеевская ночь   39
Павел Антокольский
"Мы все, лауреаты премий"   45
Александр Аронов
Стихи о странах   47
Владимир Батшев
Карелане   51
"Теперь я государству нужен"   53
Сонет Пастернаку   55
Сонет Л. К.   57
Вариация на ритмическую тему
    Иосифа Бродского   59
Сонет Г-скову   63
Пушкин на Сенатской   67
Елабуга   73
Дмитрий Бобышев
К запуску космической ракеты   75
Там был дом   79

VLADIMIR BURICH

    Confessions of a City Dweller   82

SERGEY CHUDAKOV

    Drowning   84

YURY GALANSKOV

    The Human Manifesto   86

ALEXANDER GALICH

    Ballad of the Blue Bird   96

    Conjuration   100

    Clouds   106

    Silence Is Golden   110

GLEB GARBOVSKY

    After the War   114

    Telephone Booth   118

    To the Neva   120

YEVGENY GOLOVIN

    Song of Old Party Members   122

SERGEY KALASHNIKOV

    Wife   124

    Spring in the Office   126

IGOR KHOMIN

    Idyll   130

VLADIMIR KOVSHIN

    Now That I Know   134

YEVGENY KUSHEV

    The Decembrists: *A Selection*   136

ARTYEMY MIKHAILOV

    Song About Crooks   148

    Conditions   152

Владимир Бурич
  Заповеди города   83

Сергей Чудаков
  "Когда кричат: "Человек за бортом"   85

Юрий Галансков
  Человеческий манифест   87

Александр Галич
  Песня о синей птице   97
  Заклинание   101
  "Облака плывут, облака"   107
  Молчание - золото   111

Глеб Гарбовский
  После войны   115
  Телефонная будка   119
  Неве   121

Евгений Головин
  Песня старых партийцев   123

Сергей Калашников
  Из цикла "Жена"   125
  Весна в конторе   127

Игорь Хомин
  "Дамба, клумба, облезлая липа"   131

Владимир Ковшин
  "Итак, узнав, что нужно умереть"   135

Евгений Кушев
  Декабристы   137

Артемий Михайлов
  "Хорошо быть халтурщиком"   149
  "Если ты не был в концлагере"   153

N. Nor

    To My Friends   156

Bulat Okudzhava

    Song About Stupid People   158

    Three Loves, Three Wars,

        Three Deceits   160

    Len'ka Korolyov, the King   162

    The Song of an American Soldier 166

    The Song of François Villon   168

    When We Leave   172

Yury Pankratov

    Stormy Nights   174

Muza Pavlova

    Friend   176

A. Petrov

    The Romantic Haze   178

Genrikh Sabgir

    Radio Nightmare   180

    The Death of a Deserter   184

Pavel Vladimirov

    Chapels   190

Andrey Voznesensky

    Shame   194

Aida Yaskolka

    Variations About Myself   200

Anna Akhmatova

    Requiem: A Cycle of Poems   202

    Notes   231

Н. Нор

    Моим друзьям   157

Булат Окуджава

    Песенка о дураках   159

    "А как первая любовь - она сердце
          жжет"   161

    Ленька Королев   163

    "Возьму шинель и вещмешок и каску"   167

    Франсуа Вийон   169

    "Когда мы уходим"   173

Юрий Панкратов

    Гроза ночью   175

Муза Павлова

    "Художник, нарисуй мне друга"   177

А. Петров

    "Эх, романтика, синий дым"   179

Генрих Сабгир

    Радиобред   181

    Смерть дезертира   185

Павел Владимиров

    "Стоят церквушки по Руси"   191

Андрей Вознесенский

    Стыд   195

Аида Ясколка

    Вариация о себе   201

Анна Ахматова

    Реквием   203

POETRY FROM THE RUSSIAN UNDERGROUND

Introduction
Notes from Underground

> *"All that man really needs*
> *is an independent will, whatever*
> *the cost, and whatever*
> *the consequences."*
>
> DOSTOYEVSKY

"So that's how you get these poems from Russia?"

"Yes, that's how we get them from Russia," said Alexander Ivanovich, editor of *Grani*, a Russian émigré periodical in Frankfurt am Main, Germany, which specializes in publishing Russian-language underground literature sent from the USSR.

On the table lay several "volumes" of *samizdat*—the Russian term for self-published literature—written in the Soviet Union, "published" there on typewritten sheets, and sent or smuggled to the West for "real" publication. The booklets were typed on coarse grayish paper, folded in half, and bound together by a few threads or stapled with ordinary wire used for packaging. These were the magic *samizdat* that were making headlines in the Western press, alarming the Central Committee of the Soviet Communist Party, mobilizing the Soviet Secret Police, and, eventually, condemning hundreds of people.

Samizdat is being sent to the West in many ways: by Soviet sailors visiting Western ports, by foreign travelers returning from Russia, and even by official Soviet delegations. Manuscripts may be slipped into an envelope and sent to some Western publishing house, with or without a request to have the manuscript published. A typical request might look like the one enclosed with the manuscript of Mikhail Naritsa's novel *Nespetaya Pesnya* (The Song Which Has Not Been Sung). "I beg you to transport this manuscript from our state (and the 'socialist' states also). If you do not want to do this, or there is no opportunity, burn it. But do not leave it in this country, and do not show it to Soviet critics. Watch out for thieves."

Not all authors, however, have the courage or the desire to make such a move. An author may not agree to shipping his manuscript abroad, but the nature of *samizdat* is such that once he begins circulating his manuscript (giving it to friends to read or giving it to a typist to copy) he will most likely lose control over his own work. Almost as in the Middle Ages, the manuscript, or parts of it, will be copied by the reader—who may or may not make mistakes or alterations of his own, resulting, of course, in several versions of the same text, as for instance has happened to Anna Akhmatova's *Requiem.*

The manuscripts of Solzhenitsyn's novels *The Cancer Ward* and *The First Circle* reached the West without the author's knowledge, but not necessarily against his will. Andrey Sinyavsky and Yuli Daniel sent their works abroad and asked for their publication under the assumed names of Abram Tertz and Nikolai Arzhak by publishing houses not associated with pronounced "anticommunism." Valery Tarsis, on the other hand, sent not only his manuscripts but also a photograph of himself, requesting that his works be published under his real name accompanied by his picture. Many other cases could be listed, but they would all point to the same conclusion: underground literature is not a united movement; it is carried on by individuals, and practically every case is different.

This is also true of the underground periodicals. They have most likely been "published" for home consumption, seldom with the original intention of sending them to the West. They are actually ersatz literary and political periodicals, aimed at giving others a chance to read mostly the young poets whose works, for both personal and political reasons, are not accepted by the "legal" or "official" periodicals. Most of the poems in this book have been taken from such literary "periodicals" and "anthologies," which as long as they were not suppressed, nor their editors and contributors arrested and sent to prison or labor camps, appeared more or less regularly in typewritten form.

"Why did not you try to publish your things in the U.S.S.R.?" the prosecutor asked Sinyavsky on February 11, 1966, at a session of the trial of the Soviet State versus Sinyavsky/Daniel. "As a literary critic," Sinyavsky said, "I had a pretty good idea of the prevalent tastes and standards in our literature. On a number of points they did not coincide with my taste as a writer. . . . I know the publishing business here and that is why I never submitted my things to our publishers." (*On Trial: The Soviet State versus "Abram Tertz" and "Nikolai Arzhak,"* translated, edited, and with an Introduction by Max Hayward, revised and enlarged edition, Harper & Row, Publishers, New York, 1967, p. 114.)

Sinyavsky talked only about "the taste and the norms" of Soviet publishing policy, but everybody present must have understood that he used euphemisms for two related phenomena characterizing Soviet publishing: state monopoly and prepublication censorship. Compared with nineteenth-century Russia, the USSR has made tremendous advances in fighting illiteracy and in becoming, according to UN statistics, the largest book-publishing country in the world. Paradoxically, however, the writers of contemporary Soviet society seem to be worse off in at least one respect: the nineteenth century did not know a state monopoly of publishing, even if it did know censorship. On the other hand, censorship in the nineteenth century was less sensitive and cruder than today. The seal of the censor can be found on the very last page of every Soviet book or periodical; in keeping with our technical age, it is in the form of a series of coded numbers and letters. Sinyavsky, standing trial for "violating" the unwritten censorship law, referred to these coded numbers only as "the taste and the norms" of Soviet publishing.

Others have been more outspoken. Solzhenitsyn, in his open letter to the 4th Congress of the Writers' Union in May 1967, said: "Not having access to the podium at this Congress, I ask that the Congress discuss the no-longer-tolerable oppression which our literature has endured for decades, and which the Union of Writers can no longer accept. Under the obfuscating label of *Glavlit,* this censorship—which is not provided for in the Constitution and is therefore illegal, and which is nowhere publicly labeled as such—imposes a yoke on our literature and gives people unversed in literature an arbitrary control over writers. A survival of the Middle Ages, the censorship has managed, Methuselah-like, to drag out its existence almost to the 21st century. . . . The best of our literature is published in mutilated form. . . . I propose that the Congress adopt a resolution which would demand and ensure the abolition of all censorship, open or hidden, of all fictional writing, and which would release publishing houses from the obligation to obtain authorization for the publication of every printed page." (*In Quest of Justice: Protest and Dissent in the Soviet Union Today,* edited by Abraham Brumberg, Frederick A. Praeger, Publishers, New York, 1970, p. 245.)

On April 25, 1966, at the sentencing of another underground writer, Vladimir Batshev—ironically enough the son of a high censorship official—it was stated that "From March 1964 Batshev worked as a helper at the sport-stadium . . . from May to October as a free-lance journalist for the Moscow newspaper *Moskovsky Komsomolets,* but he was fired for publicly reading poems of tendentious character. During the last half year Batshev did not work, but instead *busied himself with so-called literary activity, although he is not a member of the Writers' Union."* (*Grani,* 1967, No. 63, p. 9.)

The fight against censorship and the state monopoly of publishing, and the tutelage and monopolistic position of the Writers' Union, are central issues of contemporary Soviet literature. As Andrey Voznesensky put it in his famous protest letter of June 22, 1967: "It is not a question of myself, personally, but of the fate of Soviet literature, its honor and prestige in the outside world. How much longer will the Union of Writers go on using methods like this? Clearly, the leadership of the Union do not regard writers as human beings. This lying prevarication, and knocking of people's heads together is standard practice. This is what they do to many of my comrades. Letters often do not reach us, and sometimes replies are sent in our names. What boors, what chameleons they are! *We are surrounded by lies, lies, lies, bad manners and lies.* I am ashamed to be a member of the same Union as these people. That is why I am writing to your newspaper, which is called *Truth* [*Pravda*]." (*Problems of Communism,* September–October 1968, p. 55; italics ours.)

In 1848 Marx and Engels published their famous *Communist Manifesto,* which began with the much-quoted sentence, "A spectre is haunting Europe—the spectre of Communism." Since the death of Stalin in 1953, a spectre is haunting the communist countries once again—the spectre of freedom: freedom of the press, freedom of choice, and freedom of conscience. Yugoslavia broke with Stalin and Stalinism and became independent in 1949; Hungarian and Polish writers opened up the road of intellectual freedom further in 1953–56; in 1953–58 the struggle of communist writers in East Germany emerged. More recently we witnessed the emergence of a united front of intellectuals, writers, and even politicians in the 1968 Czechoslovak "Spring." Throughout the 1960s and early 1970s the intellectuals of Eastern Europe were joined by their Soviet counterparts—poets, writers, engineers, scientists, historians—and even by the daughter of the dead dictator. Spectres have their own logic, as Marx correctly observed, and have a tendency to become flesh and blood and demand a place under the sun.

"By the way," wrote Yury Galanskov in his open letter to Sholokhov after the latter had received the Nobel Prize for Literature in 1965, "I am also an underground writer—meant in the sense of the human underground, the sense in which Dostoyevsky expressed it. I recommend that you read him. Do you know what an underground writer is? A social-pacifist, not an underground millionaire. He does not even own a typewriter, let alone money. An underground writer works like a common laborer for a piece of bread, and he peers about, fearful that someone might disturb him. And really, the devil knows what this government is going to do. You yourself must be able to comprehend that it is difficult to be an underground author . . . an underground writer is beyond question a citizen of Russia and a man of honor, and that's why he cannot just stand by and watch the humiliation of his country and her finer sons." (*Problems of Communism,* September–October 1968, p. 58.)

Indeed, to be an underground writer in the Soviet Union is a dangerous rather than a profitable occupation; it is almost certain that the practitioner of this art will land in a jail or in a prison camp sooner or later. Why do people still do it? Sinyavsky provides us with an answer in his short story "The Graphomaniacs." There are many graphomaniacs, he says ironically, for the simple reason that there is no outlet for nonconformist literary experiments in Russia. Poems, stories, and novels which would be published in the West in little-known periodicals, often experimental and sophomoric, have no such outlets here. The frustrated authors have only one chance of reaching their fellowmen: *samizdat*. Of course this situation influences the quality of *samizdat* works, since no "natural selection" can take place; there is no way to check the reaction of the reading public toward the published works. Public approval or rejection means much to any author; they are natural guides to his further development. Even a talent of such tremendous quality as Solzhenitsyn's is affected by the lack of public reaction to his works. Reportedly, he was very much disappointed when he saw the published version of *The First Circle* and immediately decided to rework it.

This does not mean that *samizdat* automatically suggests an inferior literature; as a rule, it tends to suggest the opposite. Still, perhaps one is well advised not to idealize *samizdat* publications and to apply to them customary literary criteria in judging their quality. In our selections we attempted to look at *samizdat* poetry from this point of view, and we hope that the reader will find that many of these poems are not inferior but actually superior to much that now appears in "legal" Soviet publications.

Since the underground writer does not write for the censor, does not weigh carefully the borders of the permitted and the prohibited, it is usual to find a freshness of individual opinion, a genuine mood for experiment, a seriousness of purpose, and an urge to overcome official taboos. One can even say that if contemporary Soviet literature is readable it is because of its *underground* literature. When Western readers think of present Soviet literature, it is far less likely to be the work of such official representatives as Surkov, Fadejev, Kochetov, or even Simonov than of such writers as Pasternak, Solzhenitsyn, Bulgakov, Brodsky, Bella Akhmadulina, Yevtushenko and Voznesensky. Yet as far as most Soviet readers are concerned they are still *nonliterature*. In a very Orwellian sense they *do not exist*.

Only totalitarian ideologies believe in unanimous opinions, or that such a state of mind is desirable. The world of underground poetry—fortunately—is not homogeneous; it has no united creed, ideology, or platform. Its one uniting element is a craving for freedom, a longing for truth and moral purity, a desire to say only what man has to say, compelled by nothing except his own conscience, intelligence, and artistry. In the underground there are both political and nonpolitical writers; there are "humanists" among them; and there are those who are still communists, as well as anticommunists.

The underground consists largely of writers still in their twenties, but there are representatives of the other generations, too. Young authors such as Batshev have never experienced personally the Stalinist terror. Among the "middle generations" we find those whose youth was strongly influenced by World War II, the police terror, and the prison camps: Galich, Okuhdzhava, Sinyavsky, Daniel, Solzhenitsyn, and many others. The older generation is represented by Anna Akhmatova, Pavel Antakolsky, and, of course, Pasternak. By joining the ranks of the underground they gave it artistic maturity and, in a special sense, a public seal of approval and a strong link to the great humanistic and democratic tradition of classical Russian literature.

"The Master was dead," wrote Sinyavsky in *The Trial Begins,* and with the Master's (*khozyain*) death in 1953, and especially since the famous February 1956 "de-Stalinization" speech of Khrushchev at the 20th Congress of the Soviet Communist Party, the dead spell of that ideology was broken. The suppression of the Hungarian Revolution in 1956 embittered many, both young and old, who were looking forward to a gradual relaxation of the Stalinist practices. This was the time when the underground publications first appeared.

We know of some of these only by description. They had such titles as *The Figleaf, The Blue Bud, Fresh Voices, Culture, Heresy,* and some of the issues concerning literature revolved around enthusiastic or critical reviews of Dudintsev's novel *Not by Bread Alone,* and Yevtushenko's poetry, and the critical reexamination of the tenets of socialist realism.

Greater publicity accompanied the publication of *Sintaxis,* which managed to appear three times between December 1959 and April 1960, carrying a total of about two hundred poems by some fifty poets. The December issue was "published"—typewritten, since hectographic machines are under state monopoly and hard to come by—in an edition of three hundred copies, as was the second issue, in February of 1960, but there were only 120 copies of the third issue in April. The first issue was compiled and edited by Leningrad and Moscow poets; the second issue was devoted to Moscow poets, and the third to poets from Leningrad. It is believed that there were two later issues; these, however, have never reached the West, possibly because the editor, Alexander Ginzburg, then an unknown student of history, was arrested in September 1960 and sentenced to two years' imprisonment "for fraudulently passing examinations for others for a fee." (*Izvestiya*, September 2, 1960.) *Sintaxis*, the first underground anthology, launched the reputations of several people unknown to the West: Ivan Khabarov, Bella Akhmadulina, Bulat Okudzhava, and Joseph Brodsky.

After Ginzburg's arrest, the editorship apparently passed to another student, Vladimir Ossipov. He tried to collect the *Sintaxis* group under a new and rather symbolic name, *The Boomerang*. After three issues the periodical was confiscated and Ossipov arrested. As far as we know, none of *The Boomerang's* issues have ever reached the West.

The first widely known collection of poems appeared in 1961 under the editorship of a twenty-one-year-old student of literature at Moscow University, Yury Galanskov. *Phoenix I*, or *1961* (to distinguish it from the second issue of the periodical, which came out in 1966), presented about fifty poems by twenty-two poets, among them Pasternak's "Hamlet," the opening piece from the cycle of the *Zhivago* poems. Galanskov also included a Russian translation of Stefan Zweig's poem "Polypheme," which, of course, was meant to be a symbol of the political and poetic creed of the *Phoenix* group. Galanskov's own long programmatic poem, "The Human Manifesto," emphasized the growing impatience of this group with the Soviet establishment. N. Nor's poem "To My Friends" did the same, evoking the spectre of the revolutionary generations of the nineteenth century.

Phoenix I also contained some essays, among them an "Open

Letter to Yevtushenko" by a literary critic, Karenin, probably a pseudonym. Karenin, surprisingly, attacked Yevtushenko, who at that time was the idol of Western and, as many thought, Soviet youth. He was accused of being an "opportunist," going into an "alliance with state power," and selling out his "individual values" for "lies."

The end of *Phoenix I* came the same way as that of *Sintaxis*. After vicious attacks from Komsomol, the Communist Youth League, Galanskov was expelled from the university, arrested, and sent to a mental institution. (He died in a labor camp in 1972.) In the sixties, as we know from Tarsis' autobiographical novel, *Ward No. 7*, this treatment became an established form of political imprisonment.

With Galanskov in a mental institution and Ginzburg in prison, it took two more years until the underground was able to create a new center. It emerged in 1964, known by the capital letters SMOG. This strange word has never been defined but only interpreted as *Samoye Molodoye Obshchestvo Geniyev* (Youngest Association of Geniuses); or as *Semolst', Mysl', Obraz, Glubina* (Bravely, Idea, Image, Death); or as *Szhaty Mig Otrazhonnoy Giperboly* (Comprised Moment of Reflected Hyperbole). Among its members were Leonid Gubanov, Vladimir Aleinikov, Yuri Kublanovsky, Sergey Morozov, Yuliya Vishnevskaya, Makar Slavkov, and Vladimir Batshev.

In 1965 the moss popular "publication" of SMOG was again an "anthology" of underground poetry called *Sfinxy*. Valery Tarsis' name appeared on the title page as editor; the place and date of publication were given only as Russia, July 1965; and as "publisher" a new name appeared: ARI—*Avantgarda Russkogo Isskustva* (Avant Garde of Russian Art). For the first time the names of some very talented poets appeared "in print" and captured the imagination of readers: Alexander Galich, Yevgeny Golovin, Vladimir Kovshin, and Artyemy Mikhailov.

The year 1966 brought the appearance of a second issue of the *Phoenix* (*Phoenix II*, or *1966*), edited once again by Yury Galanskov, who after his release from the mental institution became even more active in the underground. In addition to poetry (especially by Batshev), *Phoenix II* carried several literary and political essays of great importance. There was a profound and annihilating analysis of Yevtushenko's latest apologetic narrative poem, *Bratskaya GES* (Hydroelectric Station at Bratsk), by Andrey Sinyavsky, already in prison at that time. Alexander Dobrovolsky, another well-known figure of underground literature and politics, surprised readers with a theological essay on "The Interrelation of Knowledge and Faith," in which he used mathematics to prove the existence of God. The greatest surprise for many, however, was a long treatise written by the deceased chief economic analyst of Stalin, a former Hungarian émigré, Eugen Varga. His study, "The Russian Way of Transition to Socialism and Its Results" (*Grani*, Vol. 68–89 [1967]), is the most devastating criticism of Russian economic policy during the Stalinist period that has ever come from the pen of a man professing to be a communist.

In 1965 the SMOG publications seemed to have increased geometrically. They began to assume some of the characteristics of regular publishing. This became the way in which individual poets "published" their selected or collected works. Regional anthologies began to appear, indicating that SMOG was spreading all over the Soviet Union. We know of *Yugo-SMOG* (South Smog), *Ural-SMOG*, and *SMOG-Odessa* from the Black Sea area, the traditional breeding ground of nonconformist Russian literature.

SMOG was also active in organizing political demonstrations against "re-Stalinization" and against the trials of intellectuals such as Sinyavsky and Daniel, Galanskov, Dobrovolsky, and Ginzburg, until most of the active SMOG members were themselves arrested.

Prolific as SMOG was, there were other organizations which also commanded the interest of the underground. In 1966 an independent *samizdat* magazine called *Tetrad'* (Copy Book) reached the West. Its fifth and sixth issues were dated November and December 1965. Previous numbers are not known in the West, but apparently they must have circulated in the Soviet Union. Issues No. 5 and No. 6 contained mainly fiction and political essays. It is worthwhile to mention that A. Krasnov's short story *"Na Zare"* (At Daybreak) dealt with the taboo subject of why and how people become informers for the political secret police. Characteristically enough, the hero of the story cries out at the end, "Long live freedom of conscience, and away with the abnormal profession of informer!"

Fifty years of communism in the Soviet Union has destroyed much of the national tradition which formerly bound the country—political, moral, and artistic. In exploring the world of contemporary underground poetry, one is struck by the feeling of a search for precisely that national and human tradition. Rather unexpectedly, a group of young people shows itself willing to go back as far as the beginning of the nineteenth century to find this tradition—to the Decembrist period in Russian history.

It was the period of the post-Napoleonic campaign in 1815, when victorious Russian troops returning from Paris brought back booty in their bags and revolutionary ideas in their heads and hearts. The first secret societies were organized. Isolated from the great mass of the ignorant and suppressed Russian people, an elite group of military officers and poets began to dream of a constitutional monarchy, of the liberation of the peasant-slaves, and of the victory of reason and decency over the inhuman bureaucracy. Pushkin, Ryleyev, Bestuzhev, and other great names earmark the movement, which finally resulted in the abortive uprising of December 14–15, 1825, in Saint Petersburg. The leaders were shot or sent to the gallows or to exile in Siberia. But this was the flame from which, as Lenin once said, the conflagration grew: the fire of the revolutionary movement running through the entire nineteenth century, from the Liberals of the forties to the Radicals of the sixties, the Terrorists of the seventies and eighties, and the Marxists of the nineties, on to the 1905 and 1917 revolutions.

Still, why should the Decembrists be the starting point for the new Soviet generation? To the government, it is shocking to equate the Russia of Nicholas I, the most reactionary political structure of the nineteenth century, with contemporary Soviet society. To imply that the Decembrists' dreams of constitutional democracy, the liberation of the peasants, and the victory of reason and human decency over the dead weight of bureaucracy are still to be realized is probably sacrilegious for both believing and nonbelieving communists.

No matter how shocking the parallels may be, this is the history to which a group of underground poets looks for inspiration and continuity. Yevgeny Kushev's long poem, "The Decembrists," is the most striking example of this identification. But the same concept is repeated in Vladimir Batshev's poems, and in the prison camp songs and the theoretical essays. Even Svetlana Stalina has called her generation "Decembrists who are destined to give new words and new deeds" to Russia.

But if the historical parallel is valid, then further questions must be raised. Are contemporary Decembrists willing to extend the analogy to their personal involvement and fate? It would appear that they are. Kushev expresses a deeply felt shame and pain for his generation's ineptitude and inability to reach the height of the nineteenth-century idols. Batshev, driven by similar emotions, is offering to be taken "to the accustomed place of the poet," to the gallows, as if he and the present-day Decembrists are willing to accept in advance a personal defeat and relinquish their own hopes for the success of the future. But can there be a revolution against "the country of the Revolution"? Batshev makes oblique references to the *Narodnaya Volya* (People's Will), an organization with terrorist leanings at the end of the nineteenth century. N. Nor concretizes the image of answering the unposed question in a Leninist fashion: poets exist not to become assassins but rather to be the ideologists of revolutions.

Thematically, however, the bulk of contemporary underground poetry seems to be more preoccupied with a critical survey of contemporary Soviet reality than with historical parallels about the Decembrist movement. Of course, symbols can be powerful, even if not exact. Thirty years of Stalinist rule, and the long prohibition of a critical reexamination of the past by the present rulers of the Soviet Union, have left the country with so many untold sufferings and taboos that these have become the central subject of underground poetry.

The concentration camps of the Stalinist years in which, according to conservative estimates, some twenty million people perished also figure prominently. The anonymous author (some now say that the poet is a woman) of "Etáp" depicts the day-by-day reality of the death marches, showing the way in which prisoners were driven through Siberia to their destination. The poet, however, is more than a narrator relating an event; the poem celebrates the unbroken spirit of a *zek* (Russian derogatory abbreviation for a prisoner) who faces death or the carrying out of a routine order and chooses the former. The details of the Siberian and Asiatic concentration camps which emerge from the literature of the underground sound rather familiar. We have already seen them in the classical literature of the nineteenth century, which, in restrospect, seems to be a continuous outcry against this typical Russian cruelty.

The songs of the concentration camps are different in atmosphere and theme, but they all tell about the suffering and fate of the *zeks*. Take, for example, the heart-rending farewell of the *zeks* shipped in at Port Vanin to Kolyma, the endless sadness, in which the accusation, paired with a melancholic Russian melody, creates an unforgettable impression. But there are provocatively aggressive *zek* songs, too, condemning and cursing Stalin and the Soviet regime in the foulest language, ironically mixing the vocabulary of the *blatnyje* (professional bandits) with that of the Marxist seminars in order to point to the hypocrisy of the regime.

If official sources discourage and even punish a critical reexamination of the past, then "underground" poetry does not have to observe these rules; it is deeply concerned with the question of guilt and responsibility. Andrey Voznesensky's poem "Shame" is a good example of the guilt feelings of the established poet, suffering remorse for the crimes of the fathers. Golovin's "Song of Old Party Members" charges the entire regime with the bloodshed. Antakolsky's "The Stalin Prize" deals with another aspect of the guilt: that of those who have not committed any atrocities personally but who, by silence, have made it possible for them to be committed. Galich's poem "Silence Is Golden" illuminates the same problem, not in self-defense but as an accusation. His "Conjuration" is directed against the easy existence of former secret police officers who, living comfortably on state pensions, still profess the philosophy of violence that they practiced under Stalin.

In the attempt to establish responsibilities for the crimes of the past, a rather surprising element surfaces: the invocation of religious themes. "Conjuration" is actually a chanson, each stanza of which is introduced by a prayerlike incantation, "Forgive us our sins, Lord." The hopeless entanglement of human relationships begets a spirit of metaphysical calmness and peace, rather than one of revenge for those who were wronged, and it urges penitence upon the guilty.

Any possibility of another war is painful to a generation that suffered so much during the last one. Memories of that war are still very much alive for many of these poets, especially since these events are still officially taboo. Sabgir's poem "The Death of a Deserter" recalls a shameful chapter in Soviet military history: the reign of the secret military police among Soviet soldiers during World War II. Bulat Okudzhava's antimilitary and antiwar poetry is connected with this history, although his songs are directed against all wars and all military glory. His famous "Song of an American Soldier" is of course as much about a Russian as an American soldier, and it accuses the military establishment, in general, of corrupting young people's minds with parades, irresponsibility, and the mirage of a carefree life.

The everyday reality of Soviet life is reflected in a number of poems, deeply pessimistic and often cynical. They are poems of very real alienation—a forbidden word for a communist if it is applied to his society. Artyemy Mikhailov's "Conditions" expresses the feeling that one has only a very small chance to overcome such things as the threat of the Bomb; being forced to join the "Mafia"; denouncing one's friends; living in overcrowded apartments. In "Idyll," Khomin presents a miniature picture of the typical working-class accommodations of the Stalinist era, with drunkenness, brutality, crude sexual mores, and a general social slum.

The propagandists of the Communist Party have expended much effort in teaching Russian writers the tenets of socialist realism. When Sholokhov was asked by his Czech colleagues what socialist realism was, he is reported to have said, "Go and ask Fadeyev," then the secretary of the Soviet Writers' Union, who committed suicide after Khrushchev's revelations of Stalin's crimes. A Russian émigré critic, with a good sense of humor, recommended Khomin's little "Idyll" for a study of socialist realism, truly reflected.

Poetry, of course, is not ersatz politics. Robert Frost drew a sharp line when he said that politics deals with *grievances* and poetry with *grief*. Khomin's poems, and all Russian underground poetry, should be looked at from this point of view. These poems are not "proof" of housing shortages, corrupted mores, or alienation in the Soviet Union; they convey what poetry always conveys, what Brecht called "the insufficiency of the human condition." They become political poems chiefly because they cannot be published in the Soviet Union. Thus, ironically, their "politicizing" is the result of the authorities' drive against them and not of the poets' immediate intentions.

The erosion of the values of the Party has not only such negative consequences as cynicism, alienation, and indifference, but a positive one—the search for a new beginning. Underground literature has discovered that its spiritual forerunners are the writers of the twenties and the thirties who were hunted down by Stalin. Until now, young people faced with such names as Trotsky, Bukharin, Bunin, Mandelshtam, Babel, or Bulgakov could be fed uniform and unequivocal answers; these were all enemies of the people: bourgeois nationalists, Zionists, or whatever "ism" was currently under condemnation. Stalin's death opened the Pandora's box of the past, and young people realized that the condemned were innocent victims of the terrors of twenty and thirty years before, the agonies and frustrations of which they themselves still experience. The half-hearted rehabilitation of the past had the effect of openly condemning the present.

Among the poets and writers annihilated in the Stalinist camps and prisons, Marina Tsvetayeva seems especially to have captured the imagination of the underground poets. Many poems have been written to her, by Kovshin, Akhmadulina, Batshev, and of course by her good "pen pal," Boris Pasternak. Pasternak's poems have now been published in the Soviet Union in the 1965 edition, edited and introduced by Sinyavsky just before his arrest. In a poem written in 1943, Pasternak expresses his guilt and sorrow over the news of Tsvetayeva's suicide in a Soviet concentration camp in Central Asia. The young generation also pays tribute to her and expresses feelings of guilt for crimes which they never committed. Yelabuga, the camp in which she committed suicide—that strange-sounding Tartar name—becomes, in Batshev's poem, the symbol of the unidentifiable horror which characterizes the entire Stalinist era.

Among some two hundred poets of the underground known to us so far, there are at least half a dozen names which should be mentioned individually.

Bulat Okudzhava, Georgian by nationality, Russian by education and heart, is perhaps the most original poet-bard on the literary scene; significantly enough, he cannot be fitted into the Procrustean bed of contemporary Soviet literature. Though not a socialist realist, he still is considered "realist" enough in some cases so that about half of his poems are tolerated by the official literary functionaries. The other half circulate underground.

Okudzhava is a poet, musician, singer, and prose writer. "Poetry," he has said, "for me, is always music." Okudzhava's poetry should be listened to rather than read, and his own performance, sung in a simple warm baritone voice as he accompanies himself on the guitar, is the best. Both the music and the text are simple, but they convey profound emotions. One is reminded of American folk songs, mixed with a touch of the French chansons and the traditional melancholic softness of Russian folk songs.

Okudzhava's thematic range has broadened greatly during the past few years. A decade ago, when he first gained popularity, many of his songs were about the war, such as "Len'ka Korolyov," about the good pal from the neighborhood who seemed like a king to all and went off to war and was killed senselessly. In his poems war and military exploits become little genre pictures about sadness, death, and the hopelessness of war. He is called a pacifist, a dirty word for a Soviet "patriot." But Okudzhava celebrates love, too, particularly its tragic side: women left alone by their husbands or lovers, and also the gentle feeling that only "three sisters" can redeem man—Vera, Nadeshda, and Lyubov—Faith, Hope, and Love. To Western tastes Okudzhava's love poems may appear to be sentimental; but the "real" situations, which he depicts romantically, create a painful discrepancy between the actual and the possible, and evoke feelings of longing and loneliness. Recently his themes and songs have embraced a field scorned in official literature: religion. His song of François Villon, which he performed for the first time in Paris in 1967, captures the essence of Villon's prayers; conveyed through the experience of a Soviet contemporary, the effect is unique.

Though he is not primarily a political poet, he does not hide his opinions. He is a democrat and a humanist, against all forms of oppression and manipulation.

So is another favorite of the underground, Bella Akhmadulina, of Tartar and Russian origin, the former wife of Yevgeny Yevtushenko. Her lyrics, which have roots in the poetry of the first decade of this century, remind one of the early poems of Akhmatova and Marina Tsvetayeva. Akhmadulina, like her famous forerunners, is a poet of melancholic sadness, working with real mastery of form and language. She also inhabits both the "legal" and "underground" worlds of literature. Like Bulat Okudzhava, she is basically nonpolitical, though her sincerity and uncompromising attitudes leave no doubts as to where she stands or where her sympathies lie.

Okudzhava and Akhmadulina are followers of a poetic tradition which is marked by such names as Akhmatova, Brodsky, Mandelshtam, Pasternak, and Blok. Another prominent member of the underground, Yury Galanskov, continues a literary trend closer to the Soviet tradition of Vladimir Mayakovsky. In Galanskov's "Human Manifesto" the reader is confronted with the bombastic images and rebellious alertness of a revolutionary. His revolution does not have much to do with Soviet revolutionary ideology. Paraphrasing Marx's Manifesto, Galanskov preaches the revolution of man against manipulators and demagogues. He revives the image of Christ as the symbol of universal love and redemption. For his political and literary activities he is now in a prison camp.

Anna Akhmatova's great cycle of poems, *The Requiem*, closes our volume. *The Requiem* is dedicated to the memory of the innocent victims of the Stalin era and is a human, artistic, and political document of unsurpassed quality. Akhmatova herself was a victim of the terror. Her first husband, the poet Nikolay Gumilov, was shot in 1921 for allegedly conspiring against the Soviet regime. Her son was arrested repeatedly during the great purges of the thirties, and after the war he spent many years in concentration camps. In *The Requiem*, Akhmatova expresses the deep grief of all mothers whose loved ones are lost, and she erects a literary monument to Russia's suffering. This cycle of poems was written over a period of twenty years, some of them under the influence of immediate events.

Akhmatova's *Requiem*, officially unpublished in the Soviet Union, is further proof of the shortsightedness of its present rulers. The losers are not only the poets whose work is suppressed, but also the readers at home and abroad, and most important, Russian society itself. As Solzhenitsyn said in his famous letter to the 4th Congress of the Soviet Writers' Union: "Literature cannot develop in between the categories of *permitted* and *not-permitted*, between *about-this-you-may-write* and *about-this-you-may-not*. Literature that is not the breath of contemporary society, that does not warn in time against moral and social dangers, does not deserve the name of literature; it is only a facade. In this way it loses the confidence of its own people, and its published works, instead of being read, are used as wastepaper.

"To the large public world," Solzhenitsyn's letter continued, "the literary life of our country now appears immeasurably more colorless, trivial, and inferior than it actually is or than it would be if it were not confined and hemmed in. The losers are both our country—in world public opinion—and world literature itself. If the world had access to all uninhibited fruits of our literature, if it were enriched by our own spiritual experience, the whole artistic evolution of the world would move along in a different way, acquiring a new stability and attaining even a new artistic threshold" (*In Quest of Justice*, p. 247).

With this selection of contemporary Russian underground poetry, we hope that we have made a contribution toward the fulfillment of Solzhenitsyn's hopes for literature.

TAMAS ACZEL
LASZLO TIKOS

University of Massachusetts
Amherst, 1973

ETÁP

A thousand miles, a thousand miles,
   marching until we stop
to sit in the dirt and snow and slush
   of the Siberian etáp.

And some as bleak as animals
   sat down on a breaking arch
waiting for nothing, each by himself,
   fearing the "Forward, march!"

How many hours, how many days,
   and, oh, how many years
has the dull river of that dead march
   swollen itself with tears!

But once, a bright dream in us all,
   when we were told to sit,
one bolder man, although he heard,
   just stood. And that was it.

He knew, of course, the laws and rules,
   had heard them rattled out,
and though he knew he could be shot,
   might be, without a doubt,

he acted as though he had not heard
   but followed some simple good.

Аноним

"Мы шли этапом"

Мы шли этапом. И не раз,
колонне крикнув "Стой!"
садиться наземь, в снег и грязь,
приказывал конвой.
И равнодушны и немы,
как бессловесный скот,
на корточках сидели мы
до окрика "Вперед!"
Что́ пересылок нам пройти
пришлось за этот срок!
И люди новые в пути
вливались в наш поток.
И раз случился среди нас,
пригнувшихся опять,
один, кто выслушал приказ
и продолжал стоять.
И хоть он тоже знал устав,
в пути зачтенный нам -
стоял он, будто не слыхав,
все так же прост и прям.
Спокоен, прям и очень прост,
среди склоненных всех,
стоял мужчина в полный рост,
над нами глядя вверх.
Минуя нижние ряды,
конвойный взял прицел.
"Садись! - он крикнул. - Слышишь, ты?

Over us all, bent down in the mud,
  he was told to sit. He stood.

Horizons lay in his level eyes;
  behind his eyes, the same.
Over the necks and backs in etáp
  one guard called out, took aim.

"Down!" he shouted. "You, sit down!"
  "Down!" But he would not go down.
Dark as the silence that damned us all,
  our hearts were not our own.

Like a sudden shot, the guard stood up
  and yelled out, "Forward, march!"
We straightened and trampled the mud again,
  and nobody dared to watch.

Under the sweat of our ragged packs
  our stiff necks shook with shame.
And destiny threw us in different camps.
  And nobody knows his name.

So over the serfdom of months and years
  I sing that awful hour
when a thousand men went down in etáp
  and one stood up like a tower.

Садись!" Но тот не сел.
Так тихо было, что слыхать
могли мы сердца ход.
И вдруг конвойный крикнул: "Встать!
Колонна! Марш! Вперед!"
И мы опять месили грязь,
не ведая, куда.
Кто с облегчением смеясь,
кто - бледный от стыда.
По лагерям - куда кого -
нас растолкали врозь.
И даже имени его
узнать мне не пришлось.
Но мне высокий и прямой
запомнился навек
над нашей согнутой толпой
стоявший человек.

Anonymous

CONCENTRATION CAMP SONG

Remember the port of Vanin,
the gloomy look of the sails
when we were driven aboard
those black and stinking jails.

We moved upon the waters;
the ocean's roar began,
clear to the capital
of Kolyma, Magadan.

Not songs, but bitter cries
deep in our hearts arose.
"Fair continent, farewell!"
The ship half cracked and froze.

The prisoners, feeling ill,
embraced like brothers born;
unceasing from their lips
the blackest words were sworn.

Kolyma, be damned! That they
should call you a heavenly sphere!
Here everyone goes mad;
there's no return from here.

Scurvy and Death are twain,
the hospitals sick with men.

Аноним

"Мне вспомнился Ванина порт"

Мне вспомнился Ванина порт
И вид пароходов угрюмый,
Когда нас грузили на борт
В зловонные, черные трюмы.

Над морем спустился туман,
Ревела стихия морская.
Нам путь предстоял в Магадан,
Столицу Колымского края.

Не песни, а жалобный стон
Из каждой груди вырывался.
"Прощай, материк, навсегда" -
Ревел пароход, надрывался.

От качки страдали зека,
Обнявшись, как ро́дные братья,
Невольно у них с языка,
Срывались глухие проклятья.

Проклятье тебе, Колыма,
Что названа райской планетой,
Сойдешь поневоле с ума,
Возврата оттуда уж нету.

Там смерть подружилась с цынгой,
Набиты битком лазареты,
И, может быть, этой весной
меня уж не будет на свете.

And it may happen by spring
I won't come round again.

Wife, Mother, do not cry.
My little child, look up.
That's how it is; I'll have
to empty this bitter cup.

And die. No prayer, no coffin.
Trouble is not allowed.
Here this alien snowstorm
shall lay me in its shroud.

Kolyma, be damned, you graveyard
of freedom, joy, and age!
My strength, like a guttering candle,
bows in the winter's rage.

Не плачьте ни мать, ни жена,
Ни вы, мои милые дети,
Знать, горькую чашу до дна
Досталось испить мне на свете.

Умру, похоронят меня,
И гроба не станут мне делать,
Снегами засыпет пурга,
Покроет, как саваном белым.

В метелях бушует зима
И тают свечой мои силы,
Будь проклята ты, Колыма,
Свободе и счастью могила!

ANONYMOUS

DUBROVLAG

Well, this sham trial's over, the papers fixed.
We are ready, now, to live in Dubrovlag,
rise by the bell, lie down by the bell,
counting our days of freedom.
　　Yes, that's our lot.

What are dark and light to us?
We'll clench our teeth. Why make it worse?
Or trouble ourselves with pity?
This is a special camp for you,
　　you dangerous ones.

Hours are weeks. The watchdogs slobber
under their automatic guns.
Barbed wires hum, triumph of steel.
This is a special camp for you.
　　Don't vote with your heads.

Russia, Mother, why have you been
quickened to love this death?
Here the Decembrists came as guests,
and Chernyshevsky, and those proud men
of the People's Freedom. Now, now
we come, we come; yes, we are here.
　　O Russia! Fate!

Аноним

ДУБРОВЛАГ

Суд окончен давно, и готовы бумаги.
Значит, нам суждено жить с тобой в Дубровлаге,
По сигналу вставать, дожидаться отбоя,
Дни неволи считать, дни неволи считать
        суждено нам с тобою

Здесь и днем, и в ночи мысли голову кружат,
Стиснув зубы, молчи, чтобы не было хуже,
И не мучай души сожаленьем напрасным,
Это строгий режим, это строгий режим
        для особо опасных...

Здесь порою часы, как недели, проходят,
Здесь свирепые псы, автоматы на взводе,
И колючкой не зря огорожены зоны,
Это спецлагеря, это спецлагеря
        для политзаключенных

Не жалеешь ты, Русь, арестантской баланды!
Декабристов союз угодил в арестанты,
Чернышевский был там и Народная воля,
А теперь вот и нам, а теперь вот и нам
        эта выпала доля.

BELLA AKHMADULINA

CONJURATION

No pity! I'll survive
like a beggar gone good-natured to his jail
who, from the South, bridles the chilling hail,
or like the tough sick Petersburg women in
    the postcard Southland. I'll survive.

No pity! I'll survive
like that old cripple limping at the church,
or drunk heads on the tablecloth that lurch
this way and that, or one who paints God's Mother
    under the icons. I'll survive.

No pity! I'll survive
like girls who study hard so they can read
what all this blurred-out future might concede
to pony-red hair, like mine; who'll learn my poems
    like holy fools. Yes, I'll survive.

No pity! I'll survive
and be more merciful than any nun.
And in the militant crush before I'm done,
and under my shining star—so let it burn,
    I'll manage, yes! I will survive!

Белла Ахмадулина

ЗАКЛИНАНИЕ

Не плачьте обо мне — я проживу
счастливой нищей, доброй каторжанкой,
озябшею на севере южанкой,
чахоточной да злой петербуржанкой
на малярийном юге проживу.

Не плачьте обо мне — я проживу
той хромоножкой, вышедшей на паперть,
тем пьяницей, поникнувшим на скатерть,
и этим, что малюет Божью Матерь,
убогим богомазцем проживу.

Не плачьте обо мне — я проживу
той грамоте наученной девчонкой,
которая в грядущести нечеткой
мои стихи, моей рыжея челкой,
как дура будет знать.   Я проживу.

Не плачьте обо мне — я проживу
сестры помилосердней милосердной,
в военной бесшабашности предсмертной,
да под звездой моей пресветлой
уж как-нибудь, а всё ж я проживу.

BELLA AKHMADULINA

I SWEAR

I swear by this summer snapshot
of you, lonely as a gallows
braced on the porch of a stranger,
you were driven out of that house.
That crinkled satin dress
strangles your throat,
and you sit in our past, mute
to our hunger and grief.
It's too much for a beaten horse.

I swear by this picture, by the frail
sharp elbows as small as a child's,
and by the long, drawn, dying smile
like an alibi for children.

I swear by the dark thrusts
wound in the airless griefs
and fevers of your poems,
that I, my throat bleeding,
will also cough and weep.
And I swear by this stolen image,
which I carry and never forget,
that you, a stranger, taboo,
are God's. He misses you.
I swear by your gaunt bones
crawling upon you like rat teeth,
and by holy and blessed Russia

Белла Ахмадулина

КЛЯНУСЬ

Тем летним снимком на крыльце чужом,
как виселица криво и отдельно
поставленным, не приводящим в дом,
но выводящим из дому. Одета
в неистовый сатиновый доспех,
стесняющий огромный мускул горла,
так и сидишь, уже отбыв, допев
труд лошадиный голода и горя.
Тем снимком. Слабым острием локтей
ребенка с удивленною улыбкой,
которой смерть влечет к себе детей
и украшает их черты уликой.
Тяжелой болью памяти к тебе,
когда, хлебая безвоздушность горя,
от задыхания твоих тире
до крови я откашливала горло.
Присутствием твоим крала, несла,
брала себе тебя и воровала,
забыв, что ты - чужое, ты - нельзя,
ты - Богово, тебя у Бога мало.
Последней исхудалостию той,
добившею тебя крысиным зубом.
Благословенной родиной святой,
забывшею тебя в сиротстве грубом.
Возлюбленным тобою не к добру
вседобрым африканцем небывалым,
который созерцает детвору.

who forgets your deep asylum,
and by that bastard out of Africa
watching over the children,
and the children, by Tversky Boulevard,
and by the sad peace of a heaven
lacking profession and pain.

I'll kill your Yelabuga
and let the new grandchildren sleep,
even though the mothers of mothers
frighten them there in the evenings,
whispering, Yelabuga! she lives!
  "Child, sleep; be still
    Or the blind Yelabuga comes!"
It is ready now! It's coming!
It is stumbling! Quickly, quickly!
And I bring down my boot with its nails
hard on its stretching fingers,
and hard on its throat, and keep
the weight of my heel to its tip.

I swear by the children its blood
will burn my feet like green poison,
and I'll throw to this bottomless earth
the ripe green egg of its tail.
But not one word of that porch

И детворою. И Тверским бульваром.
Твоим печальным отдыхом в раю,
где нет тебе ни ремесла, ни муки.
Клянусь убить Елабугу твою,
Елабугу твою, чтоб спали внуки.
Старухи будут их стращать в ночи,
что нет ее, что нет ее, не зная:
"Спи, мальчик или девочка, молчи,
ужо придет Елабуга слепая."
О, как она всей путаницей ног
припустится ползти, так скоро, скоро.
Я опущу подкованный сапог
на щупальцы ее без приговора.
Утяжелив собой каблук, носок,
в затылок ей - и продержать подольше.
Детенышей ее зеленый сок
мне острым ядом опалит подошвы.
В хвосте ее созревшее яйцо
я брошу в землю, раз земля бездонна,
ни словом не обмолвясь про крыльцо
Марининого смертного бездомья.
О, в этом я клянусь. Пока во тьме,
зловоньем ила, жабами колодца,
примеривая желтый глаз ко мне,
убить меня Елабуга клянется.

where Marina, homeless, died!
And I swear, though our Yelabuga
should fix me with yellow eyes
and swear in the dark, in the stench
of swamps, by the toad of spring,
that it will kill me. I swear!

BELLA AKHMADULINA

BARTHOLOMEW NIGHT

Once, in a cozy rainy hour, while thinking,
it dawned upon me, suddenly, that a child
born near bloodshed is thought to be immoral.
This is well known, although the legend's wild.

That night when the holy saint, Bartholomew,
threw a big party for the greedy ones, how thin
must have been the cries of children between fires:
whether the Huguenots or the Catholics let him in.

That newborn lamb, who could not even walk,
that little baby, singing his nonsense sounds,
survived and learned to take his early airs
from the last breaths on the executioners' grounds.

Nanny, no matter now how much you nurse
your child with the flowery milk of mead and win
the lifestreams in his own pure little blood;
in him there lives an alien oxygen.

He loves his sweets; he wants to nurse again;
but nothing in that body knows the bloat
that's grown unsatisfied, with vehemence,
from inhaling the foul air of a cut throat.

But he gets used to breathing; he can't be blamed.
With what catastrophe religion stung

Белла Ахмадулина

ВАРФОЛОМЕЕВСКАЯ НОЧЬ

Я думала в уютный час дождя:
а вдруг и впрямь, по логике наитья,
заведомо безнравственно дитя,
рожденное вблизи кровопролитья.

В ту ночь, когда святой Варфоломей
на пир созвал всех алчущих, как тонок
был плач того, кто между двух огней
еще не гугенот и не католик.

Еще птенец, едва поющий вздор,
еще в ходьбе не сведущий козленок,
он выжил и присвоил первый вздох,
изъятый из дыхания казненных.

Сколь, нянюшка, ни пестуй, ни корми
дитя твое цветочным млеком меда,
в его опрятной маленькой крови
живет глоток чужого кислорода.

Он лакомка, он хочет пить еще,
не знает организм непросвещенный,
что ненасытно, сладко, горячо
вкушает дух гортани пресеченной.

Повадился дышать! Не виноват
в религиях и гибелях далеких.
И принимает он кровавый чад
за будничную выгоду для легких.

and claimed its bloody miracle! He cries
for the everyday advantage of his lung.

I know not in what shadow or whose bones
he sleeps, or what his cozy childhood seems,
but both the hangman and the hangman's victims
heavily watch that baby's lidded dreams.

And when his eyes are opened, will he see?
How will that poison take him? Could we tell?
Will he be glad? Or pleased to die, or kill?
Or smother away in slavery, as well?

Good people, more accustomed than I am
to death in its abundance, personal war,
the way you coddle children tells me still
you're not afraid of what your children are.

And if a child should cry out in his sleep,
or toss in nightmares in his trundle bed,
don't worry; only his gums have been disturbed
by the sweet tooth of blood-milk in his head.

If something ghostly from the outer branches,
grotesquely chewing, chills you to your spine,
don't be afraid; it is the face of children
who sucked the heavy silk of bloody wine.

It may be that some spirits out of heaven
can take those cries in honor, as a choice,
and lavish, still, upon such fragile natures
of small throats crying still another voice

Не знаю я, в тени чьего плеча
он спит в уюте детства и злодейства.
Но и палач, и жертва палача
равно растлят незрячий сон младенца.

Когда глаза откроются - смотреть,
какой судьбою в нем взойдет отрава?
Отрадой - умертвить? иль умереть?
Или корыстно почернеть от рабства?

Привыкшие к излишеству смертей,
вы, люди добрые, бранитесь и боритесь,
вы так бесстрашно нянчите детей,
что и детей, наверно, не боитесь.

И коль детя расплачется со сна,
не беспокойтесь - малость виновата:
немного растревожена десна
молочными резцами вурдалака.

А если что-то глянет из ветвей,
морозом жути кожу задевая -
не бойтесь! Это личики детей,
взлелеянных под сенью злодеянья.

Но, может быть, в беспамятстве, в раю,
тот плач звучит в честь выбора другого,
и хрупкость беззащитную свою
оплакивает маленькое горло

to hide them from the horror for a while,
enchanted by that music, like as not.
But then, of course, this is a small affair
of thirty thousand, who were Huguenot.

всем ужасом,чрезмерным для строки,
всей музыкой, не объясненной в нотах.
А в общем-то - какие пустяки!
Всего лишь - тридцать тысяч гугенотов.

PAVEL ANTAKOLSKY

THE STALIN PRIZE

We all are winners of that prize
granted to us, in His name,
defended by His chilly eyes
  and our uneasy fame.

    Fellow soldiers of the Man,
    harboring our local fears,
    we kept the silence, as we can.
      Crimes done through the years.

Hiding from each other's friends,
sleepless in each other's nights,
we all were chosen for His ends,
  the hangman of our rights.

    We who sought "eternal" themes,
    reasoned axioms and wise,
    have Lublyanka for our dreams
    and blood behind our eyes.

Children's children, if you do
heap contempt upon our name,
none of us, no matter who,
  would try to hide his shame.

    This guilty rhythm of the head
    comes down to simple choice:
    we hated, yes, the One now dead,
    but most, our silent voice.

Павел Антокольский

"Мы все, лауреаты премий"

Мы все, лауреаты премий,
Врученных в честь него,
Спокойно шедшие сквозь время,
Которое мертво.

Мы все, его однополчане,
Молчавшие, когда
Росла из нашего молчанья
Огромная беда.

Таившиеся друг от друга,
Не спавшие ночей,
Когда из нашего же круга
Он делал палачей.

Мы, сеятели вечных, добрых,
Разумных аксиом,
За кровь Лубянки, тьму допросов
Ответственность несем.

И пусть нас переметит правнук
Презрением своим,
Всех одинаково, как равных -
Мы сраму не таим.

Да, очевидность этих истин
Поистине проста.
И не мертвец нам ненавистен,
А наша немота.

ALEXANDER ARONOV

A LITTLE GEOGRAPHY

Although it sounds strange,
maybe
there are other countries on our planets:
  The Sovereign Nation of Musicians,
  The Heterodoxy of Empty Heads,
  of Fat Bellies, or Dull Minds,
  The Far Country of Lovers,
  of Fire Fighters, of Jazz Labor Heroes,
  The Democracy of Clever Ones,
  The Soviet of the Stupid Ones.
Labels!
      You know
           who is who.
You've seen it, haven't you?

If not, read it
in all the papers:
The Republic of Readers and the Republic of Writers
are breaking off diplomatic relations.
  What a sensation!

People are drowning
in the Country of the Swimmers!

Now the travelers are sitting,
frustrated.

Алексадр Аронов

Стихи о странах

А, может, и будут, как это ни странно,
На свете такие различные страны:
Страна Скрипачей
и Страна Трепачей,
Страна Толстяков
и Страна Простаков,
Страна Влюбленных,
Страна Пожарников
и маленькая Республика Джазовых Ударников,
Страна Мудрецов
и Страна Дураков.
Прописка -
            и ясно, кто ты таков.

- Читали или нет? Прочтите обязательно!
Газеты публикуют важное сообщение:
Страна Читателей и Страна Писателей
Порывают дипломатические отношения.

- Какое наслаждение! Спешим со всех концов!
Случилось наводнение
В Стране Пловцов!

- Сидят,
никак не достанут виз,
мучаются отчаянно
путешественники

They have no visas from
The Country of the Brown Noses
   into
The Really Big Bosses.

Hello! Aren't you a Dandy?
   Of course I am.
I'll be damned, we're countrymen!

Good-bye, Mother; so long, Father.
I'm leaving
        for the Southwest
and a distant land,
The Empire
      of beautiful
            seventeen-year-old
                girls.

из Страны Подлиз
В Государство Больших Начальников.
— Хэлло, вы не Пижон?
— Пижон.
— Мы земляки! Я поражен!
До свиданья, мама,
До свиданья, папа,
Я уезжаю
          на Юго-Запад
В страну, отдаленней которой нет:
Красивых Девчонок Семнадцати Лет...

VLADIMIR BATSHEV

VOICES

If I hear no voices call,
there are hands upon this wall.

When my own lips turned aside
there the other voices died.

Well, forget it. I will call
from Lefortovo to you all.

If no voice from cell and block
echoes, still you'll hear me knock.

Do you hear my knocking? Yes,
imprisoned in these sentences.

Now I have to leave you, dumb
where Octobers never come.

Shadowy steps surround me. Live
and love me. If you can, forgive.

And if you can, please get away,
and burn this poem. This I say.

Lefortovo Prison
March 5, 1966

Владимир Батшев

КАРЕЛАНЕ

Если голоса нет -
руки есть на стене.

Губы есть в стороне -
только голоса нет.

Ты об этом забудь -
я тебя позову.

Если голоса нет -
постучу по стене.

Слышишь, слышишь мой стук -
приговоры несут.

Мне уходить от тебя
осенью без октября.

Гул шагов не затих.
Если можешь - прости.

Если можно уйти -
ты сожги этот стих.

5 марта 1966
Лефортовская тюрьма

VLADIMIR BATSHEV

NOW THE STATE NEEDS ME

It's spring, and the State needs me.
The light burns all night long;
In the mirroring glass of the lamps
fear walks in unreality. . . .
Then what, what can I say?
From the green throat of my cell
only the walls are coughing.

This. That now a cunning dream
lets down its bars, dripping
water like stepping guards
tapping along the gutters;
and on the floors the little
observation flaps
click to their own applause and
to the moans in the dank walls.
Well, nothing will come of it.

And the day is hard, hard.
Secrets hide in these stones,
and also people. A thaw
comes to my small window.
I'll break it; it strangles my collar!
Yes, the eyes of Lefortovo
and these bars are burning. Spring,
what are you saying now?

Lefortovo Prison
March 6, 1966

Владимир Батшев

"Теперь я государству нужен"

Теперь я государству нужен -
не гасят ночью свет.
И лампочку не тушат
в зеркале-стекле,
Всё чудится, всё кажется...
О чем мне вам рассказывать?
Здесь только стены кашляют
зеленым горлом камеры,
вот сон придет коварный,
свободный, без решеток...
И, как шаги конвойных,
капе́ль стучит по желобу,
и, как аплодисменты,
глазок стучит на двери,
и стоны в мокрых стенах...
Не на что надеяться.
А день тяжел и труден.
А за стеною тайны.
А за стеною люди.
А за окошком тает...
Рвануть, как ворот, форточку:
весна, чему научишь!?
Горят глаза Лефортово
решетками наружными.

6 марта 1966
Лефортовская тюрьма

VLADIMIR BATSHEV

SONNET TO PASTERNAK

And now the bridges carved in wood are burned,
the bridges which for all these years we kept
in Petersburg. His Marburg, lo, has turned
into unloving country while we slept.
Four strings, four Muses, now have fallen off;
there where he raised up three wherever he went,
above those strings this smoky spring will scoff
and tear at the four walls of imprisonment.
The great brow of Acropolis resounds
like voices in a picture, bright with May;
and a necrologue of rust cries in those grounds
that a lifeblood of the Litfond passed away.
I go there still, and by his tombstone bow,
for I am small. We all are smaller now.

Владимир Батшев

СОНЕТ ПАСТЕРНАКУ

И мосты, как дрова, сожжены...
Те мосты столько лет поминал
Петербург. - Марбург свой поменял
На кусок нелюбившей страны.

Оборвутся четыре струны,
Там, где три на виду подымал,
А над струнами дым и май
Обломают четыре стены.

Не аукнут аккорды Акрополя,
Как и голос с посмертного фото,
Лишь прошамкает ржавый некролог,
Что скончался "один из Литфонда".

Я приду. Поклонюсь памятнику.
Помолюсь. Я ведь маленький-маленький.

VLADIMIR BATSHEV

SONNET TO L.K.

How often that our yesterdays
talk to the ghosts of other rooms,
and chairs and portraits find their ways
among the lampshades of those tombs.
They hang upon the light of years
like daylit gliding parachutes
and drift upon our hopes and fears,
miserable in our attributes.

So let them talk in silence still.
Do not forget, or hurry home;
they still review your book of shame,
though they have forgotten, as they will,
from where your patronymics come,
your painful loneliness, your name.

Владимир Батшев

СОНЕТ Л.К.

Как часто ночью говорят
Предметы комнаты вчерашней.
Вот этот стул, портрет навязший
В зубах, и абажур, как маскхалат,

Висит уж сколько лет подряд,
Как будто парашют парящий,
О чьей-то помощи просящий,
Хоть этой помощи не рад.

Пусть говорят они в тиши.
Перебирая твои даты.
Домой идти ты не спеши,

Ты знаешь, то, что не отдали
Тебе больного одиночества,
Забыв об имени, об отчестве...

VLADIMIR BATSHEV

VARIATIONS ON A THEME
OF JOSEPH BRODSKY

I am engulfed in white fog,
and the snows have melted long ago.
It is hard; I am tired; I keep moving.
Bukovsky is still free,
but I do not even know him.
And I have just slipped out of town
and am living at a dacha with a friend.
This is a hot summer; it's 1963.

I'm fooling around with girls,
some lovely and some not.
And there in the meadow cows
are chewing upon the grass.
I'm insignificant now;
my poems are poorly written,
but I keep on reading the papers
and I'm scared.

Soldiers shuffle the roads
under their blue epaulets.
There is something sweaty about their faces
and their hands; it's the hot
summer of 1963.

The fog keeps spreading and spreading,
but my friends and I are buddies;

Владимир Батшев

ВАРИАЦИЯ НА РИТМИЧЕСКУЮ ТЕМУ
ИОСИФА БРОДСКОГО

Белый дым стелится надо мной.
И белый снег давно растаял.
Но мне очень трудно. Я изнемог,
и я себя по местам расставил:

еще на свободе Буковский,
но я не знаком с ним даже
я только что вырвался из города.
Я у друга моего живу на даче -
жаркое лето
63 года.
Я ухаживаю за девочками:
они хорошие и плохие.
На лугу пасутся коровы
и жрут травы.
Я еще очень маленький
и совсем плохо пишу стихи я.
Но я читаю газеты,
и мне становится страшно.
По шоссе проходят военные.
На их плечах синие погоны,
их лица и руки чем-то липким клеймены...
Жаркое лето
63 года -
мы с... еще лучшие друзья,
и мы победить клянемся.

we swear that we will win.
I just got a job in a factory,
and I know, deep down, what the workers
think, and all the people, too.
More and more I keep asking,
"What would happen if . . . ?"

Still, I am insignificant.
I know so very little.
I have to keep moving,
be going somewhere always.
I want to change my Russia
and bless her with things not yet seen.
Visions appear: the Decembrists,
and those of the Narodovoltsy.

I am jealous of Bukovsky;
though he is a stranger to me.
Maybe it's better that way.
I don't know what will happen tomorrow.
Maybe that's why this bitterness
has been in my mouth since the first night.

So I praise poems
wailed by a tomcat. . . .
I am insignificant.
And this is the hot summer
of 1963.
And now I am making my way,
I am making my way to the gallows.

Я уже работаю на заводе.

В душу рабочего

и всего народа я проникаю,

все чаще я задаю себе вопрос:

"А что будет, если?.."

Но я еще маленький.

Я ничего не знаю.

И мне надо ехать.

Опять куда-то ехать!

Я хочу изменить Россию,

дать ей что-то такое невиданное,

мне мерещатся декабристы, народовольцы, путчи.

Я завидую Буковскому.

Я ему очень завидую,

но я его не знаю,

и это, может быть, лучше.

Я не знаю, что будет завтра.

И наверно от этого, а не от неуменья

у меня во рту после первой ночи горько.

Я расхваливаю стихи,

которых еще кот наплакал...

Я маленький.

Жаркое лето

63 года -

я дорогу свою выбираю,

я выбираю свой путь на плаху.

VLADIMIR BATSHEV

SONNET TO G——OV

Your dark reflections, in the night,
for five long minutes let you dwell.
To you, alone, they do not lie;
and being there, they simply tell

the utter truth: that your concerns
are not for them, who cannot know
the ways your agitation burns
or how your inspirations go.

And they'll still come another day
to cord your throat with webs of frost.
You'd better wear a warmer hat.

The road through town is long and gray
and difficult, when one is lost.
They're coming now. Remember that.

❁   ❁
❁

Well, we always have to start at the beginning,
trying to put the pieces together,
and not from some chance clay.
Ask always, yes,
for true answers; say

Владимир Батшев

СОНЕТ Г-СКОВУ

Твои ночные отраженья
приходят не на пять минут.
Они одни тебе не лгут
и говорят без промедленья

всю правду. И твое волненье
здесь не оценят, не поймут
они тот обнищавший труд,
что выдаешь за вдохновенье.

Они придут. А новый день
морозом остужает горло.
Ты шапку теплую надень.

Тебе идти сейчас по городу
так долго. Очень труден путь.
Они приходят - не забудь.

* * *

Всё надо начинать сначала:
осколки склеивать,
а новое
лепить из глины не случайной,

you want views and reviews. Remember
whom we caress.
Our cause
is no prescription for the blind alleys
pretending to be avenues.

Yes, I got tired, Commander of the Laws.
Inscribe, "Defeat!"
I fell asleep on guard this past December.
Remember?
I grew weak.
So cut me down
as one, today, would snip a shock of hair
from underneath his cap.

Enough, enough!
Close up this empty year:
   faces in the lime trees,
   falsifications
   under a flight of daws. . . .
Send me off, sir,
Commander of the Laws,
to join the poets in their most
accustomed places.

не доверяясь голословным
ответам,
отзывам,
рецензиям,
и понимать,
Кого

ласкаем.
Ведь наше дело по рецептам
нельзя составить, как лекарство.
Переулки сегодня длинней,
всем проспектам они подражают.
Командир, запишите мне
поражение.
Я уснул на посту в декабре.
Я устал.
Я из сил выбился.
Вы сегодня меня обрежьте,
словно чуб, из-под шапки выбившийся.
Довольно.
Закройте пустой календарь,
где лица,
где липы,
где галок полеты...
Переведите меня, командир,
на старое место поэта.

VLADIMIR BATSHEV

PUSHKIN AT THE SENATE SQUARE

I

Olympus is destroyed
and Pegasus made lame. . . .
Listen, Natalya, your
fireplace has no flame.

Above the cripples' graves
the crosses march as one;
a rebellious carré,
by fate, still leads you on.

But what is it to you,
the rebellion they led?
The new year at its end?
All those bodies dead?

It's easy to grow old
when the guards hold in place,
well hidden in the crowd,
your own beloved's face.

II

Looking out of the window,
you want to grow old, old.

Владимир Батшев

ПУШКИН НА СЕНАТСКОЙ

I

Разрушился Олимп
и охромел Пегас...
Послушай, Натали,
твой камелек погас!

Над кладбищем калек
кресты подняли бунт:
мятежное каре
решит твою судьбу.
А что тебе они?
Зачем тебе мятеж?
И новый год поник
под грузом мертвых тел.
Нетрудно постареть,
увидев пост столиц.
А где-то в том каре
любимый твой стоит.

II

Ты смотришь из окна,
ты хочешь постареть,
как неизвестный знак
мерцают на стене
о, тени мертвецов! -
ты их не пережил.

The unfamiliar shadows
of bodies cold, cold,

flicker the twilit walls.
Oh, you shall not survive
in the soul's frailty,
broken and drowned alive.

Hide all your poems in
forgotten tables. Moans
compel you to the Square
where blood runs on the stones.

Whether we still might live
in simpler personal wars,
who knows? Of course it would
be simpler to kill the czars.

But you are a poet, and
the Square is rumbling, gone
in blood. A pistol comes,
shouting, "You are the one!

"You are the wildest one!"
By those hard words I'm stung.
We all know that Ryleyev
from the gallows swung.

И сломано весло
оплеванной души.
Запрячь свои романы
в забытый стол,
тебя на площадь манит
кровавый стон,
беда бежит на площадь:
быть иль не быть?
А может это проще:
царей убить?
Конечно, это проще.
Но ты - поэт!
А площадь кровью ропщет
и дарит пистолет,
кричит: "Ты самый левый!
На мельницу не лей..."
Ты знаешь, что Рылеев
качается в петле,
ты знаешь, что поэты
в Сибири за ножи...
Хоть шлешь ты им приветы,
но ты-то жив!
Побыть бы здесь подольше,
но огненный рысак
тебя увозит дальше -
тебе пора писать.

And in Siberia, poets
march to the bayonet. . . .
Perhaps a greeting sent
may prove you are living yet.

A fiery carriage comes
and carries me toward night.
Should I have stayed there longer?
No, it is time to write.

III

In April or May would songs
or sonnets cease to dare
the Mayakovsky Place,
or the old Senate Square?

Remember this and the dead
movement of hands, like wings.
The frozen bush breaks,
and the troubled woodcock sings.

III

Ты вспомнишь эту площадь
и мертвый взмах руки,
когда в холодной роще
защелкают курки.
В апреле? В мае? кончатся
сонеты и сонаты.
И площадь Маяковского
станет нам Сенатскою.

Vladimir Batshev

YELABUGA

The monks are white in Yelabuga.
Pure are the orange-colored painters
staining the window lights with dancers
in old and burnished monasteries.

Holy with texture of jams and lamplight,
the primitive cupolas glow in polished
golden icons of Yelabuga,
high in the sky-blue monasteries.

Владимир Батшев

ЕЛАБУГА

А в Елабуге белые старцы
и оранжевые маляры
разукрасили белым танцем
голубые монастыри.

Разукрасят вареньем и лампами,
купола от ожогов стары.
На лубочном боку Елабуги
голубые монастыри.

DMITRY BOBYSHEV

UPON THE LAUNCHING OF A SPUTNIK

What a rotten life this is!
And the whole damn world's like that.
The five o'clock robots mob the newsstands;
in the post office the workers' hands are calloused,
sorting out letters;
and we municipal garbage collectors
puke in the backyards.
There's no free food yet,
and no free clothes.

O universal emptiness
and empty universes,
we are zooming another Sputnik
into another planet,
probably to a hard landing.
So that's man!
For a short hitch he eats and makes love,
but even the young kids
launch from their mother's breast
with a cosmological finger.

Hey, tell me, where the hell
should a garbage collector live?
Should I double my back to gather calluses?

Дмитрий Бобышев

К ЗАПУСКУ КОСМИЧЕСКОЙ РАКЕТЫ

Как мало жить!
А все стоит земля.
А все толпятся у газет рабочие.
Себе наращивают мозоля
От писем

         служащие почты.

И за отгруженными дровами
Играют дворники в биллиард.
А ведь жратва еще не даровая,
И не бесплатна выдача белья.

Но нет - людей все пустота пленяет,
И приспособлены нарочно скорости
О заграничные планеты
Расплющивать живые кости.

Вот человек!
На столь короткий срок
Ему отпущено любви и хлеба.
Ан грудь отталкивает сосунок
И тычет пальцем в небо!

А где, скажите, дворник проживает?
Где горб и мозоли наживает?
Где метлы и щетки,
Лопаты его и скребки?

And where are my food and clothes?
Don't I pick up the filth of the whole bloody town,
eh? So that's man?
Free, once in a while, for an hour
in all his sickly fears?

O you magnificent failures,
poking around in your heavy uniforms
in dark and smelly hallways,
why don't you ever repair the goddamn place
and help clean the kitchens
and their filthy cans?

At least I'm a true collector of garbage,
and I, too, have a rage to live.

Ему работы до чорта
Доставят окурки и коробки.
А человек!
На сколь короткий срок
Тебе отпущены безумства и болезни.
Ты неудачный времени сынок,
Бредущий по разбитой лестнице.

Так починяй перила на земле
И ремонтируй дворнику жилье.
Он проживает тоже на земле
И честно моет и скребет ее.

DMITRY BOBYSHEV

A HOUSE WAS THERE

A house was there
on the far
shore.
Then soldiers stopped
for a smoke.

A house was there,
and people, too.
Then soldiers came.

Before they came
the morning was quiet
and children sang through the day.

But the soldiers broke
the trunks of the trees
and burned their roots
in a green smoke.
One of them sang.
He had wounds on his body.
They opened their rations
and noisily ate.

And then they smoked
their cigarettes,

Дмитрий Бобышев

ТАМ БЫЛ ДОМ

Там был дом,
на другом
берегу.
У солдат был там перекур.
Там был дом.
Люди жили в нем.
А солдаты пришли потом.
Перед этим.
Утром — тихо. А днем
пели дети.
А солдаты шли по дороге,
видят — дом.
У деревьев сломали ноги,
разожгли с трудом.
Слушали, как один поет —
через тело шрамы —
разворачивали паек,
шелестели, жрали.
Покурили. Потом огонь
притоптали своей ногой
и ушли.
И конец на том.
Там был дом.
Там
был
дом.

stamped out the fires
and rose and left.

And that's that.
A house was there. . . .

A house
was
there.

VLADIMIR BURICH

CONFESSIONS OF A CITY DWELLER

Yup, I mean yes, sir,
sure, I always switch the light off when I leave.
No, I don't jaywalk, and you know
I always look to the left, middle, and right
before I cross. Naturally I watch out for cars.
I am also very wary of falling leaves.
Don't smoke, don't argue, don't drink,
and I always wash my fruit, sir,
and boil my water.
Really, I drink nothing but champagne
and a few juices.
After every single meal I wash my hands.
Oh, yes,
before I go to sleep
I brush my teeth.
Me? Why, I would never read in bed
with a poor light.
Yes, that's precisely what I've been doing
for twenty-six years.
Now what do you think I should do next?
Put my money in a savings bank?

Владимир Бурич

ЗАПОВЕДИ ГОРОДА

Уходя, гашу свет.

Перехожу улицу на перекрестках.

Сначала смотрю налево. Дойдя до середины -
    направо.

Берегусь автомобиля.

Берегусь листопада.

Не курю.

Не сорю.

Не хожу по газонам.

Фрукты ем мытые, воду пью кипяченую.

Пью шампанское и натуральные соки.

После еды мою руки.

Перед сном чищу зубы.

Не читаю в темноте и лежа.

Так дожил до двадцати шести лет.

И что же?

Хранить свои деньги в сберегательной кассе?

SERGEY CHUDAKOV

DROWNING

When midsea travelers cry,

                    "Man overboard!"
the ocean liner, bright as a storied tower,
plows to a halt
and the submerged man

                    is fished efficiently out.

But when the soul

                    falls overboard,
when man is drowning in blue fear

                    and deep despair,
then not even his humming apartment house

                    stops in the troubled wake,
                    but floats through the anonymous air
                    and drifts away.

Сергей Чудаков

"Когда кричат:"Человек за бортом!"

Когда кричат:
                "Человек за бортом!"
Океанский корабль, огромный, как дом,
Вдруг остановится
И человек
             веревками ловится.

А когда
           душа человека за бортом,
Когда он захлебывается
         от ужаса
           и отчаяния,
То даже его собственный дом
Не останавливается
                и плывет дальше.

YURY GALANSKOV

THE HUMAN MANIFESTO

1

More and more in the quiet of the night
I begin to cry;
it seems impossible to give anyone the richness—
not even a small morsel—of the soul.
Nobody needs it,
though day by day you break
searching for Idiots!
And men, after their eight hours,
go moonlighting
or chasing women.
What does it matter?
I ride the human flood
like a stranger, alone,
a ruby
glittering among icebergs.
Sky,
let me shine, let me sprinkle
the jewels of my soul in the night
upon a dress of black velvet.

2

Ministers, officials, newspapers— Who believes them?
Rise up, you beaten people, look!
Eyeballs of nuclear death

Юрий Галансков

ЧЕЛОВЕЧЕСКИЙ МАНИФЕСТ

1

Всё чаще и чаще в ночной тиши
вдруг начинаю рыдать.
Ведь даже крупицу богатств души
уже невозможно отдать.
Никому не нужно:
в поисках Идиота
так измотаешься за день!
А люди идут, отработав,
туда, где деньги и бляди.
И пусть.
Сквозь людскую лавину
я пройду, непохожий, один -
как будто кусок рубина,
сверкающий между льдин.
Небо!
Хочу сиять я.
Ночью мне разреши
на бархате черного платья
рассыпать алмазы души.

2

Министрам, вождям и газетам - не верьте!
Вставайте, лежащие ниц!

glow in the graves of the world.
Arise!
Arise!
Arise!
O, the purple blood of revolutions!
Get up; tear down
that rotten prison of a state!
Climb on the bodies of cowards
with black bombs like dark plums
for the bright hunger of people,
serving them in the stone plates of public squares.

3

But where are they all,
those people we need
to dive in the throats of guns
and hallow the sores of war
with the holy knives of rebellion?
Where are they?
Where?
Oh where?
Or were they never there?
Oh yes, they were chained to machines, shadows
begging the pittance of money.

Видите - шарики атомной смерти
у мира в могилах глазниц.
Вставайте!
Вставайте!
Вставайте!
О, алая кровь бунтарства!
Идите и доломайте
гнилую тюрьму государства!
Идите по трупам пугливых
тащить для голодных людей
черные бомбы, как сливы,
на блюдища площадей.

3

Где они -
те, кто нужны,
чтобы горло пушек зажать;
чтобы вырезать язвы войны
священным ножом мятежа.
Где они?
Где они?
Где они?
Или их вовсе нет? -
Вон - у станков их тени
прикованы горстью монет.

4

And now those men are gone.
Zilch, like a fly,
they stir and die in the papers.
I dash out into the square
and shove myself into the ear of the town
yelling my despair. . . .
Then, getting my gun,
I hold it hard and cold against my temple. . . .
Let no one trample
the snow-white flag of my soul.
Don't stop me, people!
I don't want you.
Who needs
your consolations?
I cannot breathe your hell
or greet corruption and hunger!
Lying upon the ground,
I curse your iron cities
filled with cash and filth.

4

Человек исчез.
Ничтожный, как муха,
он еле шевелится в строчках книг.
Выйду на площадь
и городу в ухо
втисну отчаянья крик...
А потом, пистолет достав,
прижму его крепко к виску...
Не дам никому растоптать
души белоснежной лоскут.
Люди!
Оставьте, не надо...
Бросьте меня утешать.
Всё равно среди вашего ада
мне уже нечем дышать!
Приветствуйте Подлость и Голод!
А я, поваленный наземь,
плюю в ваш железный город,
набитый деньгами и грязью.

5

Sky,
what am I doing?
Give me the avenging knife!
Look, where some bastard
splashed black lies upon white.
Look, how the shadow of dusk
chews
on a blood-spattered banner.
Life is a prison
built on a terror of bones.
I am falling!
I fall!
I am falling!
I am done. Go, all of you; grow bald.
Not me.
Why should I chew this shit
as you, all of you,
do?
I will not pillage graves
to drive my hunger down.
And I will never knead your bread
watered with tears. No.
Now, falling and drifting away,
I feel that all things human
blossom again, in me,
in a half-sleep, in a half-dream. . . .

5

Небо!
Не знаю, что делаю...
Мне бы карающий нож!
Видишь, как кто-то на белое
выплеснул черную ложь.
Видишь,
как вечера тьма
жует окровавленный стяг...
И жизнь страшна, как тюрьма,
воздвигнутая на костях.
Падаю!
Падаю!
Падаю!
Вам оставляю лысеть.
Не стану питаться падалью -
как все.
Не стану кишкам на потребу
плоды на могилах срезать.
Не нужно мне вашего хлеба,
замешанного на слезах.
И падаю, и взлетаю
в полубреду,
в полусне...
И чувствую, как расцветает
человеческое
во мне.

6

Walking along the streets
through leisurely hours
one comes to be accustomed
to the dark twisted faces.
Then, all of a sudden, there
like a clap of thunder,
like the new revelation of Christ,
arises
the crushed and crucified light
of man.
It is—me,
calling to Truth and Rebellion,
a serf no more,
tearing the black wombs
woven with lies.
It is—me,
chained by the Law,
yelling this Human Manifesto!
Let the black ravens now
peck out
on my cold white body
the Cross!

6

Привыкли видеть,
расхаживая
вдоль улиц в свободный час,
лица, жизнью изгаженные,
такие же, как у вас.
И вдруг -
словно грома раскаты
и словно явление миру Христа -
восстала
растоптанная и распятая
человеческая красота.
Это - я,
призывающий к правде и бунту,
не желающий больше служить,
рву ваши черные путы,
сотканные из лжи.
Это - я,
законом закованный,
кричу человеческий манифест!
И пусть мне ворон выклевывает
на мраморе тела
крест!

BALLAD OF THE BLUE BIRD

Oh, once I was stupid and strong,
and a blue bird filled my dream.
I found its blue tracks before long—
for fifteen years, so they seem,
for fifteen, right or wrong,
and the banner of blue was supreme.

It wasn't like soldiers we died
but numbers that lied and lied;
Karaganda to Narym and more,
our land was a running sore.
Vorkuta, Inta, Magadan—
who thought such a fate for a man?
The plague of the scurvy? You heard?
And the *zeks* from the Party a third!
Oh, red were our bannering fears
that were slapping on ten more years.

Then war took over that world
with its dark yellow banner unfurled.
While women wept in their doors
those camps went straight to the wars.
Sevastopol, Kursk, and in Brest
a yellow glow blinded our West,
and the yellow one faded to white
but stayed in our eyes like the night.
Oh, the yellow has ruined us all;

Александр Галич

ПЕСНЯ О СИНЕЙ ПТИЦЕ

Был я глупый тогда и сильный,
Все мечтал я о птице синей,
А нашел ее синий след -
Заработал пятнадцать лет.
Было время за синий цвет
Получали пятнадцать лет.

Не солдатами - номерами
Помирали мы, помирали.
От Караганды до Нарым
Вся земля как один нарыв.
Воркута, Инта, Магадан,
Кто вам жребий тот нагадал?

То вас шмон трясет, а то цынга,
И чуть не треть зэка из цека.
Было время - за красный цвет
Добавляли по десять лет.

А когда пошли миром грозы -
Мужики на фронт, бабы в слезы.
В желтом мареве горизонт,
А нас из лагеря да на фронт.
Севастополь, Курск, город Брест,
Нам слепил глаза желтый блеск.
А как желтый блеск стал белеть,
Стали глазоньки столбенеть.

we can't tell the air from a wall.
And now we are crippled and dumb.
Was it Dalton where all this began?
Some colors don't go with some.
How the hell do we know where we ran?
So let's drink to this kingdom come.
We all are a Dalton man.

So figuring life and our lot,
let us guess at the color we got.

Ох, сгубил ты нас, желтый цвет,
Мы на свет глядим, а света нет.
Покалечены наши жизни,
А может, дело всё в дальтонизме?
Может, цвету цвет не чета,
А мы не смыслим в том ни черта?
Так подчаливай, друг, за столик!
Ты дальтоник, я дальтоник.

Разберемся на склоне лет,
За какой мы погибли цвет.

ALEXANDER GALICH

CONJURATION

Forgive us our sins,
O Lord,
forgive us our sins!

Now that he has his personal pension,
he has come for an hour to a bar like this,
the Floating Bar that smells of clamshells
and a ceiling of patches like puddles of piss.

The shashlik rises with the taste of candles,
and the waitresses, smelling of codfish, are free.
Oh, he should have sat down at the bank of the river
instead of in here at this den by the sea.

O you sea, sea, sea, Black Sea,
You screwed-up guy, he began,
You don't seem to go by the books,
Part Cain and part Abel, part man.

Forgive us our sins,
O Lord,
forgive us our sins!

On the shore where nightfall is filled with couples
he was wandering, furious, gloomy, alone,
muttering, "Beastly! This Black Sea is stupid.
It allows itself more than has ever been known."

Александр Галич

ЗАКЛИНАНИЕ

Помилуй мя, Господи, помилуй, мя!..

Получил персональную пенсию,
Завернул на часок в "Поплавок",
Там ракушками пахнет и плесенью,
И в разводах мочи потолок.
И шашлык отрыгается свечкою,
И "сулгуни" воняет треской,
И сидел бы он лучше над речкою,
Чем над этой пучиной морской.

Ой ты, море, море, море, море Черное!
Ты какое-то крученое-верченое!
Ты ведешь себя не по правилам,
То ты Каином, а то ты Авелем!

Помилуй мя, Господи, помилуй мя!

И по пляжу, где под вечер по́ двое,
Брел один он задумчив и хмур.
Это Черное, вздорное, подлое
Позволяет себе чересчур.
Волны катятся, чортовы бестии,
Не желают режим понимать!
Если б не был он нынче на пенсии,
Показал бы им кузькину мать!

The waves splashed at him. "You sons of bitches!"
Whatever their orders, they sure didn't know.
If only he still had not been retired
he would show them what's what and where they could go.

> *O you sea, sea, sea, Black Sea,*
> *Neither zek nor defendant, tonight*
> *I would roll you to Inta for "Kontra,"*
> *And from Black I would turn you to white.*

> *Forgive us our sins,*
>> *O Lord,*
> *forgive us our sins!*

Back in his lodgings, and drowsing, he saw
the whole Black Sea guarded well by the cops,
and the terrible waters, as strange as his dream,
all marching to Inta, and all in *etáp.*
He was happy as those who are blessed in Christ,
and with a cigar, *Mayak* in his mouth,
he watched the good *vokhrovets*—fellows to you—
slapping black waters in barracks down south.

> *O you sea, sea, sea, Black Sea,*
> *The law gave you into my hands;*
> *We've mastered a couple of tricks*
> *To use on you guys in our lands.*

> *Forgive us our sins,*
>> *O Lord,*
> *forgive us our sins!*

Ой ты море, море, море, море Черное!
Не подследственное, жаль, не
                заключенное!
На Инту б тебя свел за дело я,
Ты б из Черного стало Белое!

Помилуй мя, Господи, помилуй мя.

И в гостинице странную, страшную
Намечтал он спросонья мечту:
Будто Черное море под стражею
По этапу погнали в Инту.
И блаженней блаженного во Христе,
Раскурив сигаретку "Маяк",
Он глядит, как ребятушки вохровцы
Загоняют стихию в барак.

Ой ты, море, море, море, море Черное!
Ты теперь мне по закону порученное!
А мы обучены для этой химии,
Обращению со стихиями!

Помилуй мя, Господи, помилуй мя!

И лежал он с блаженной улыбкою,
Даже скулы улыбка свела.
И должно быть, последней уликою
Та улыбка для смерти была.
И не встал он ни утром, ни к вечеру,

He lay there, serene, with a smile on his face,
the tips of his mouth running up to his ears;
he might be the corpus delicti of death
if we all can be lucky as he with our fears.
Came morning and evening, he never got up,
and the maid got a doctor to come to his bed
and lit a small candle to put at his head.
Oh, the hangman was happy, but dead, dead, dead.

O you sea, sea, sea, Black Sea,
May you murmur and ever be free
And never behave by the rules,
Being Cain and part Abel, and me.

Forgive us our sins,
O Lord,
forgive us our sins!

Коридорный сходл за врачом,
Коридорная Божию свечечку
Над счастливым зажгла палачом.
И шумело море, море, море Черное,
Море вольное, никем не прирученное,
И вело себя не по правилам,
Было Каином и было Авелем!

Помилуй мя, Господи, в последний раз...

ALEXANDER GALICH

CLOUDS

Clouds are flying, are flying,
swimming slowly as in movies.
But I have a butt in my mouth and
am draining a bottle of vodka.

Flying to Abakan,
they swim along so slowly
it seems they are sweating in heaven
and I, though I'm living, am frozen.

My boots are at zero in sleigh tracks
and ice that I scratched with my ax;
oh, it wasn't for nothing that twenty
years laid me out in those camps.

Eyes still aching from snowlight,
always I hear the guards yelling,
"Somebody get the pineapple
and another big bottle of vodka!"

Clouds are flying. They fly to
My favorite spot, my Kolyma;
no one will need any lawyers;
they couldn't care less about mercy.

I'm living first class and exchanging
my twenty hard years for some pennies,

Александр Галич

"Облака плывут, облака"

Облака плывут, облака,
Неспеша плывут, как в кино.
А я цыпленка ем табака,
Я коньячку принял полкило.

Облака плывут в Абакан,
Неспеша плывут облака,
Им тепло, небось, облакам,
А я насквозь продрог на века.

Я подковой вмерз в санный след,
В лед, что я кайлом ковырял,
Ведь не даром я 20 лет
Протрубил по тем лагерям.

До сих пор в глазах снега наст,
До сих пор в ушах шмопоган
- Эй, подайте мне ананас
И коньячку еще 200 грамм!

Облака плывут, облака
В милый край плывут, в Колыму.
И не нужен им адвокат,
И амнистия им ни к чему.

Я и сам живу - первый сорт,
20 лет на пятак разменял,

sitting in pubs like an English
lord, and I even have teeth now.

Eastward the clouds still are flying.
No trouble in getting my pension:
one letter comes on the fourth
and the twenty-third brings me another.

Nowadays, one half of the country
is sitting, like me, in the bars,
and upon the screens of our memories
dark clouds fly at the stars.

Я в пивной сижу, словно лорд.
И даже зубы есть у меня.
Облака плывут на восход,
Им ни пенсии, ни хлопот,
А мне 4-го перевод
И 23-го перевод.

И по этим дням, как и я,
Полстраны сидят в кабаках.
Нашей памятью в те края
Облака плывут, облака.

ALEXANDER GALICH

SILENCE IS GOLDEN

We are all getting big. Oh, it's lovely
to no longer be fools like a child
running out to the fairy-tale islands
or the lost lands beyond the old sheds.

No one's now going to the North Pole
or to the Sahara in boats or on bicycles.
Gold is the rule of our silence. Naturally,
all of us students are eager to learn this.

   If you shut your mouth you'll be rich,
   So let's button, button our lips.

Oh, we trust neither heart nor mind here,
nor make any choices. We play it all safely.
What could be better than silence now,
never to be against but always for something?
And where are those who spoke of their doubting?
They sang in their youth, and now they are rotting,
and those who were silent are living and ruling.
It's as we were saying: Silence is golden.

   If you shut your mouth you'll be rich.
   So let's button, button our lips.

Александр Галич

МОЛЧАНИЕ — ЗОЛОТО

Мы давно называемся взрослыми
И не платим мальчишеству дань,
И за кладом на сказочном острове
Не стремимся мы в дальнюю даль.
Ни в пустыни, ни к полюсу холода,
Ни на катере к этакой матери,
Но поскольку молчание - золото,
То и мы, безусловно, старатели.

 Промолчи - попадешь в богачи.
 Промолчи, промолчи, промолчи.
И не веря ни сердцу, ни разуму,
Для надежности спрятав глаза,
Сколько раз мы молчали по-разному,
Но не против, конечно, а "за".
Где теперь крикуны и печальники?
Отшумели и сгинули смолоду,
А молчальники вышли в начальники,
Потому что молчание - золото.
 Промолчи - попадешь в богачи.
 Промолчи, промолчи, промолчи.
И теперь, когда стали мы первыми,
Нас заела речей маята.
Но под всеми словесными перлами
Проступает пятном немота.

Now that we've made it and we are the Chosen
maybe we seem to be talking too freely,
but under our flowery phrases we're keeping
a silence that's louder than any we're speaking.
We let all the others cry out, despairing;
let them be humble and chilly with grieving.
The rest of us know that silence is better;
it's as we were saying: Silence is golden.

Oh, it's simple now to be rich,
and simple to be the top dog.
Here Simple, the Hangman, comes,
so let's button, button our lips.

Пусть другие кричат от отчаянья,
От обиды, от горя, от холода,
Мы-то знаем - доходней молчание,
Потому что молчание - золото.

    Вот как просто попасть в богачи,
    Вот как просто попасть в первачи,
    Вот как просто попасть в палачи -
    Промолчи, промолчи, промолчи.

GLEB GARBOVSKY

AFTER THE WAR

First the buffalo
dwindled into their dusty reservations,
and here and there a hippopotamus
vomited its sour waters;
next the scurvy goats stumbled in scrub brush
and the wire-thin legs of flies withered
even as their wings whirred;
and statuesque rhinos
broke in their serrated horns
and cracked in their stiff legs and caked hides.
Domestic dogs went wild,
the cancerous virus began to fail,
and the last man vanished.

All earth lay under the thickening snow;
in equatorial zones
its chilling crystals shone,
and African tides stood still in a deep blue ice.
Hoofs and the long steel runners and spun treads
stalled in their hides and sleds and cars
under the gathering snow,
until only a few colossal chimneys
poked an ancient and blackened finger
coldly into the sky.
Then gravity, itself, fell sick,
heaved in its corpse, and died.

Глеб Гарбовский

ПОСЛЕ ВОЙНЫ

Сначала вымерли бизоны
на островках бизоньей зоны.
Потом подохли бегемоты
от кашля жуткого и рвоты;
козули пали от цынги,
у мух отнялись две ноги
(но мухи сразу не скончались),
дикообразы вдруг легли -
еще колючие вначале -
но вот обмякли, отошли.
Оцепенела вдруг собака,
последним умер вирус рака,
потом скончался человек...
На землю выпал плотный снег;
снег на экваторе искрился,
снег в океане голубел,
но санный след не появился,
и шинный след не проскрипел...
Машины снегом заносило,
чернели трубы - пальцы труб;
земля утрачивала силу,
все превращалось в общий труп;
и только между Марсом, правда,
и между умершей Землей
еще курили астронавты
и подкреплялись пастилой;

Still in their chromed asbestos suits
lounged between Earth and Mars,
the cosmonauts puffed away our silver filters.
Precisely on the hour
they dialed for physical fitness, filled out the forms,
and theoretically sat down,
relics in a pure room.
Called back in their timeless days,
no one was answering.
Still on their shadowless autoerotic switches
all those pretty little red and green control lights
blinked and beeped and twinkled.

сидели молча, как предметы,
с Землей утратившие связь,
и электрического света
на пульте вздрагивала вязь...

TELEPHONE BOOTH

Here the transparent booth
>   sits in its walls of glass.
And now, if you wish to arrange
>   a date for the evening ahead,
if you want to accost your friend
>   with a long and longer talk,
or if you want to fight it out
>   with somebody called your wife
until your mouth is fuming
>   and your stiff backbone is cracking,
then go ahead! About life,
>   or death, or whatever you want,
you can shout it all in the phone;
>   it's free, and maybe it's good.
But you hear the people knocking
>   on the glassy wall with their coins,
"Time's up; time's up; time's up. . . ."

Глеб Гарбовский

ТЕЛЕФОННАЯ БУДКА

Прозрачная будка, стеклянные стены.
Хотите назначить свиданье на вечер,
хотите на друга обрушиться с речью,
хотите с женою ругаться до пены,
до пены у рта, до ломоты хребта -
        пожалуйста!
О жизни, о смерти, о чем вам угодно,
кричите по проводу, благо - "свободно",
пока не ударят монеткой в стекло,
пока наше время - не истекло.

TO THE NEVA

River, what if I never return
                    when I'm still young!
What then?
How shall I be with the Neva
and the girls floating beside me
                    like icebergs
as if I ever were
indifferent. . . .
River, what if I never return
                    still young!
How should I smile with an old mouth?
Will rheums and skeletons in rubber shoes
waver where the quilted jackets
                    from stark camps
catch my youth in the fog?

Even so, I will surely return,
                    believe me;
I will have that,
at least that much
                    for all these years.
I will come back, no matter what,
even if, when I do return,
                    I'm dying.

Глеб Гарбовский

НЕВЕ

Я могу не вернуться к Неве

молодым...

Что тогда?

Как держаться тогда с Невой?

Будут девушки мимо меня,

как льды,

проплывать,

точно я - не свой,

безразличный девушкам,

им...

Я могу не вернуться к Неве молодым...

Как тогда улыбаться ей

старым ртом?

Ревматическим костяком

как тогда без галош,

без снабженного ватой

глухого пальто

обгонять в туман

молодежь?

... Я вернусь к тебе

верящим -

мне дано -

мне дано это много

на годы впредь...

Я вернусь к тебе любящим

все равно,

даже если вернусь

умереть...

YEVGENY GOLOVIN

SONG OF OLD PARTY MEMBERS

To Yuri Stepanov

The faces and slogans are one,
but they snag in October's chains;
our flags, like the torches of Nero,
   flame in the rains.

We drink to us all. Red Star,
bow down, just a bit, your eye.
We'll strum on the old guitar.
   Let them watch the sky.

Let the slaves of rules and laws
crawl in their shadowy gloom.
Who cares if the blood-red posters
   their slogans resume?

Our forefathers proudly kept
their health with a different good.
But those mausoleum stones
   are clotted with blood.

Евгений Головин

ПЕСНЯ СТАРЫХ ПАРТИЙЦЕВ

Ю. Стефанову

Все, как прежде, ни лица, ни стона,
Скованные цепью Октября,
Как живые факелы Нерона
Красные полотнища горят.

Веселится молодой и старый,
Пять когтей разнежила звезда.
Струнами чудовищной гитары
Натянулись в небе провода.

И рабы привольных конституций
Вылезли из всех своих углов.
На багровых лозунгах смеются
Зубы наших заповедных слов...

Раз отцы не сберегли здоровья -
Мы добудем счастье всех людей,-
Где осколком затвердевшей крови
В мостовую впился мавзолей.

SERGEY KALASHNIKOV

WIFE

From a Cycle of Poems

In the third year of married life,
the fourth from the moment we met,
I got tired as hell of it all,
the tears,

      the speeches,

           the threat.
In the third year of married life
I am utterly washed out and done.
Where is my courage now
to be always coddling that one?
It is love, not pain, that I want,
the liquor of lost belief,
in the third year of married life
and the thirtieth month of grief.

Сергей Калашников

Из Цикла "Жена"

На третьем году супружества,
четвертом - с момента встречи,
осточертели до ужаса
слезы,

      угрозы,

            речи.
На третьем году супружества
я, именуемый мужем,
не нахожу в себе мужества
лелеять одну и ту же.
Хочу любить, а не тужиться,
и тянет пропиться до нитки
на третьем году супружества,
тридцатом месяце пытки.

SERGEY KALASHNIKOV

SPRING IN THE OFFICE

The day as usual. The office working.
In every chair a girl is sitting.
Seeing nothing and hearing nothing.
Beyond the window spring is flitting.

Just yesterday, on all the fences
the starlings made their own connections,
and next to the red-brick office building
a puddle changed the snow's complexions.

In all that crowd one girl delighted
that puddled water with playful capers
by folding pigeons from her memos
and flying them out of the endless papers.

Just run away with the fresh winds blowing!
Earth, in its inner core, is naked!
The Voice from the Inner Office called, and . . .

.   .   .   .

The very next morning she heard these fragments:
not performing duties, they say . . .
neglecting to come to meetings . . . missing
the International Women's Day.

Сергей Калашников

ВЕСНА В КОНТОРЕ

Дела идут, контора пишет,
в конторе девушка сидит.
Она не видит и не слышит,
как за окном весна гудит.

Еще вчера на всех заборах
скворцы налаживали связь,
а возле здания конторы
большая лужа разлилась.

Хотелось девушке беспечно
пускать кораблики по ней,
а из инструкций бесконечных
бумажных делать голубей,

умчать туда, где ветер крепкий,
земля гола до черноты...
Но кто-то канцелярской скрепкой
. . . .
А утром дали ей взысканье
за то, что допускает лень
и не явилась на собранье
в Международный Женский День.

And all these fragments turned to firing.
She heard it all, yet all her heart sensed
was blue sky when the sun was shining,
and not this Personnel Department.

Again the black roofs through the window.
Again she sees the ice is going.
The day as usual. The office working.
And down the wind her salary blowing. . . .

Когда приказ подшили в дело,
хотелось от тоски кричать...
На бланке неба

         солнце тлело,
как чья-то круглая печать.

Опять в окне чернеют крыши,
на крышах тает мокрый лед...
Дела идут, контора пишет,
кассирша деньги выдает.

IGOR KHOMIN

IDYLL

I

Flowers and flowerbeds and a stunted poplar
huddle around the sheepbarn apartments.
And down the long corridor
eighteen families awaken to slogans:
  Peace to the World!
Out in the courtyard, Ivanov,
the accountant for national loans,
is smoking the bedbugs out of their clothes.
The Makarovs are drunk and raising hell,
and the Baranovs are having a family fistfight.

II

To Yuri Vasilyev

Caviar, fish, and wine
in the shopwindow shine.
Behind the window Inna waits
for another evening with a room,
table, and couch with her husband drunk,
shouting, "To hell with it all!"
He grunts and snores like a pig,
and Inna cannot sleep.
Again in the morning shine
caviar, fish, and wine.

Игорь Хомин

"Дамба, клумба, облезлая липа"

Дамба, клумба, облезлая липа.
Дом барачного типа.
Коридор. Восемнадцать квартир.
На стене лозунг "Миру - мир".
Во дворе Иванов
Морит клопов.
Он бухгалтер Госзнака.
У Макаровых пьянка.
У Барановых драка.

Ю.Васильеву

Рыба. Икра. Вина.
За витриной продавец Инна.
Вечером иная картина:
Комната, стол, диван.
Муж пьян.
Мычит: Мы-бля-я...
Хрюкает, как свинья,
Храпит.
Инна не спит...
Утром снова витрина.
Рыба. Икра. Вина.

III

He asked her up for a minute
to put a new record on,
and then he locked the room.
She rushed to the door and froze
stock-still in the screaming silence,
and the groaning and crying
was drowned by the record.

IV

Somebody threw out the garbage,
splashing the brown dishwater;
somebody scrawled a face on a fence
and scribbled, "This is Zoia."
Quarreling down in the barn, fists already flying.
It's holiday; it's the first of May.
. . . The entire house is bored.

Пригласил ее в гости.
Сказал: потанцуем под патефон.
Сам дверь на замок.
Она к двери, там замок.
Хотела кричать, обвиняла его в
        подлости.
Было слышно мычанье и стон -
Потом завели патефон.

Кто-то выбросил рогожу,
Кто-то выплеснул помои,
На заборе чья-то рожа. -
Надпись мелом: "Это Зоя".

Двое спорят у сарая,
А один уж лезет в драку...
Выходной. Начало мая.
Скучно жителям барака.

VLADIMIR KOVSHIN

NOW THAT I KNOW

Now that I know I am surely coming to die,
as a day dies, with light in our trees and hair,
I see, as a stone or a leaf, one mute cold law:
when we go, willy-nilly, we shut the door.

Why should my body lie open again and again
like a battered sign in a taverned bitch of a slum?
Take all your chaos and noise; I've had that grind!
And isn't it time? So go, go lock my door,

and leave me, at nightfall, utterly mute and dumb.

Владимир Ковшин

"Итак, узнав, что нужно умереть"

Итак, узнав, что нужно умереть,
как умирают дни: светло и верно,
я понимаю - истина примерна
и время двери закрывать.

Зачем же вновь, зачем же все опять,
как вывеска разлапистой таверны,
шумливо, спутано и скверно?
Не время ль двери закрывать?

YEVGENY KUSHEV

THE DECEMBRISTS
A Selection from a Cycle of Poems

1. RYLEYEV

Poems go up in smoke again, and wind
blows them about the city streets. Men,
it isn't the first mistake that you have made.
Why are you sticking your young necks out again?
Choke down your high emotions. Hold yourself
in readiness and drink some more. Why bang
your head upon the heavy world, my boy?
You will be broken on the wheel; you'll hang—
an exhibition on the picture walls.
Do you not see the gallows where they stand
inviting us as neighbors, disciplined,
while all the planets of the universe
laugh at our feet down-dangling in the wind?

Now only God can save us; now we know
that if men save they do it like a dunce;
they'll drag us by our heads before the crowds
and all our friends deny us all at once.
The crows will harshly cry, "They hatched a plot,"
and no policemen say a word but "Yes!"
And they will burn us like the very plague. . . .
Perhaps it is too early to confess.
Perhaps we should get on with it. Yes. Yes.

Евгений Кушев

ДЕКАБРИСТЫ

1. РЫЛЕЕВ

А стихи пойдут на цигарки...
А поэмы развеются в улицах...
Ты уже не раз ошибался -
Так чего же, мальчик, бунтуешь?
Подавляй, подавляй свои чувства!
Подливай, подливай в стаканчик!
Но уже всё на свете чуждо.
Против всех ты бунтуешь, мальчик.
Обломают, а тело вывесят,
Как рисунок для обозренья.
Видишь виселиц чудо-выставку?
Будем мы с тобой соседями.
Посмеются планет созвездия,
Как ногами мы станем покачивать.
Нам от Бога только спасение,
От людей - одни лишь проклятия.
Нас с тобою потащат волоком,
И друзья зараз отрекутся.
- Эти мальчики - скажет ворон
Поперхнулись на Революции.
А жандарм ничего не скажет.
И сожгут нас, точно заразу...
Только рано, наверное, каяться,
Может, стоит ещё попытаться...

7. JULY 13, 1826

The capital still sleeps.
At dawn the guard is changing.
Impassive faces freeze.
An icy wind is raging.
God knows, one wouldn't think
that criminals were made
just for the sake of the show.
To hell with this masquerade!
Now Colonel Sukin thinks,
counting himself alive,
that chained hands cannot live:
One, two, three . . . five!

Who can believe it now,
five noblemen gone down,
good jobs and lovely wives,
for the riffraff of the town,
the peasant and the tramps?
Whom did they think to bless?
What for? I do not know.
The guns freeze, motionless.
And there in the biting wind
Commander Sukin came
and raised a white cloth up.
"Poet? His fate's the same;
his head is also draped
with the same sack." Six o'clock,

Утро. Рано. Спит столица.
Но сменился караул.
Застывают злые лица
На растерзанном ветру.
"Не узнали б, Бога ради,
Что преступников казнят!
К чёрту эти маскарады!
К бесу, к бесу эту казнь!"
Думает полковник Сукин
И считает про себя
Цепью скованные руки:
"Первый...

      двое...

           трое...

                пять!

Непонятно! Все - дворяне.
Есть и служба и жена,
А пошли во имя рвани,
Плебса, нищих и хамья.
Что им, грешным, больше нужно?
А зачем? Нет, не пойму!"
Стынут люди, стынут ружья
На растрепанном ветру.
А начальник этот, Сукин,
Раз за беленький платок -
"Всё ж поэт, а тоже участь,
словно нимб, на нем мешок!"

while over the populace
the bells of morning sound,
and Sukin, in charade,
leads his precise parade.

8. THE EXILED

Russia, your honor chills
and freezes like tears in the wind.
The exiles, rather than march by themselves,
go dragged and blind.
Three guards? Six guards?
A whole detachment? We don't care.
Siberia, we give you to them;
take them, anywhere!
Torture and cripple them,
and let them die in that condition;
the pines are monsters there,
the taiga born to endless inquisition,
and glittering under the stars,
the snow like diamonds in dust. You knew,
Decembrists, Decembrists,
what was in store for you.
You didn't break, confess,
or give in; and your poems, like fragile words
we say again, those chains
uprising into swords.

Шесть часов.

       Туманность.

              Утро.

Горожане сладко спят.
Господин начальник Сукин
казнь проводит, как парад.

8. КАТОРЖАНЕ

Честь России, как слезинка,
Застывает на ветру...
Вот идут они слепые,
Не идут, а их ведут
Три жандарма,

           шесть жандармов
Или целый эскадрон.
Ты бери, Сибирь - не жалко!
Мы тебе их отдаем!
Измотай их, изувечи, -
И помрут они тогда.
Сосны - это изуверы,
Инквизиция - тайга.
Снег под звездами искрится
Изумрудами в пыли...
Декабристы, декабристы,
Знали вы, на что пошли!
Не раскаялись, не сдались,
А крамольные стихи,
Словно цепи, для восстаний
Переплавим на штыки!

9. THE MONOLOGUE OF A GENDARME

Those ensigns and those first lieutenants
were taught a lesson for their pains.
We hanged them high to prove our words.
They got the chains, the chains.

Only five of them were hanged
in the roaring wind alive.
But it was absolutely fate
that the others should survive.

Now let these silly youngsters come
and keep this Senate Square.
Now let them. We are all alert
as even the walls are.

We learned our jobs, oh, well indeed,
and by experience taught,
and in the chains of history
freedom and honor caught.

Let them teach their poems to sing,
if they can teach them how,
since they are lined upon the walls
and hanged and stiff by now.

Listen, I'll tell you frankly now
that truth resides in power;
the warrants for their own arrests
were signed within the hour.

9. МОНОЛОГ ЖАНДАРМА

Корнеты и поручики
проучены, проучены.
Словам моим порукою —
наручники, наручники.

Повешено лишь пятеро
под ветра гимн.
Совсем не обязательно
оставить жизнь другим.

И пусть смешные мальчики
смотрят на Сенат.
Мы теперь внимательны.
Мы — стена.

Делам жандармским учены,
и опыт есть.
Наручники, наручники
на волю, честь.

Пусть всякие поэтишки
поют про свой Парнас.
Повешены, повешены
они уже сейчас.

Я говорю вам искренне,
что в силе — правда есть.
Подписаны, подписаны
приказы на арест.

Everything is prepared ahead:
the hangman and the jail,
the exile suited to command,
and honored without fail.

We are the guardians of the State,
The silence of the land.
Of Pechorins we're unafraid;
or of Muravyev's hand.

Our loyal gendarmes, rank on rank,
surround us and atone.
Who would dare disturb the czar
or his majestic throne?

Meanwhile, well-fed and satisfied,
we're all things possible.
We are the hunting dogs; our work
is indispensable.

The hunting dogs are loyal still,
more sensitive than you;
for when the critics fail and fall
so will the hangmen, too.

Готово всё заранее:
тюрьма, палач, острог.
Любое мы задание
исполним точно в срок.

Мы - государства стражи.
Мы - тишина в стране.
Печорины не страшны,
а Муравьевых нет.

Служителей у трона
несметное количество.
Кто посмеет тронуть
покой Его Величества?

А пока насыщенно
мы ходим там и тут.
Мы - сыщики. А сыщика
необходимый труд.

Он верный, исполнительный
и чуткий, как Орфей.
Когда не будет критиков -
не будет палачей.

А если не получится -
наручники, наручники...

10. THE EPILOGUE OF A POET

I dream of armies rioting my sleep,
particularly when December comes,
and then I take my place in Senate Square
in strict formation with the guns and drums.

And here I am at once met by
Ryleyev, Pavel Pestel, Bestuzhev,
and utterly and silently
by Pyotr Kakhovsky and Muravyev.

Then, almost like fathers to my soul,
impassive, quietly suffering, and lonely,
they whisper to me, "Tell us, is it true
that you inherited the whip, only?

"And is it true our hatred of the hangman
is still passed on and kept by you?"
What can I answer? What can I answer them?
My tears obey the silence. "Yes, it is. . . ."

10. АВТОРСКОЕ

Мне сны тревожные снятся...
Особенно в декабре.
Тогда иду на Сенатскую
И становлюсь в каре.

И тотчас меня окружат
Молча, без всяких слов,
Рылеев, Пестель, Бестужев,
Каховский и Муравьев.

А после, словно по-детски,
Спросят они меня:
"Правда, что вам в наследство
Досталась только петля?

Правда, что лишь Некрасов
Да наш богемный поэт
Счистили черную краску,
Нас переделав в свет?

И что через сотню с лишним
Битых годов кнутом
В каждом русском мальчишке
Есть декабря огонь?

Что перешла по наследству
Ненависть к палачу?"
Что я могу ответить?..
Заплачу... и промолчу...

Artyemy Mikhailov

SONG ABOUT CROOKS

Hey, look!
How great to be a crook.
They are always so smartly clad,
and just think of the girls they have had.
And in addition, and this is really a smash,
they've also got the cash.
Just in case you never happened to sup with them,
let me tell you that things are changing so fast
    nowadays that only a crook can keep up with them;
one day we are praising corn on the cob, and the next
    it's apt to be squash;
therefore, neither can be had in the market unless
    you just happen to be flush.
Indeed, whether you do or don't go by the book,
it's so great to be a crook.

You talk about counterfeiters? They're so innocent
    it isn't even funny;
they forge only money.
But what about those others who forge our highest ideals,
as though patriotism and humanism and truth and
    democracy and poetry and history and even bread
    and love were merely idle panaceas!
Oh, a crook is an easygoing fellow;
some of them are downright mellow.

Артемий Михайлов

"Хорошо быть халтурщиком"

Хорошо быть халтурщиком.
Веселые они всегда, сытые,
Хорошо одеты.
И деньжата у них есть, и девочки.
И всегда они идут в ногу со временем.
Теперь ведь все так быстро меняется,
Что только халтурщик не отстанет:
Сегодня кукурузу хвалили, а завтра брюкву.
А потому нет ни того, ни другого.
Хорошо быть халтурщиком.
Фальшивомонетчики - самые невинные из
                                халтурщиков -
Они только деньги подделывают.

А эти - самые высшие ценности:
Патриотизм и человеколюбие,
Истину и демократию,
Стихи и историю,
Любовь и хлеб...
Легконоги они, халтурщики,
Куда ветер подует, туда и они.
Подлое перекати-поле, несутся,
А подует обратный ветер,
И здесь они впереди всех,
Пенкосниматели.

Like dandelions obeying the prevailing wind,

they go where it goes and, therefore, have never even sinned.

And should that wind suddenly blow from the opposite direction

they are the first to change, since this is their only intention.

Even among tailcoats and silk,

they skim the cream off milk.

And since they have nothing to overestimate

they are successful and gay.

Indeed, wherever you look,

they are loved by hook and by crook.

Ведь им нечего переоценивать,
А потому они всегда веселые и
                            удачливые.
И все их любят.

CONDITIONS

Tricked by your dearest friend,
trapped and dragged to a camp,
tortured and drugged,
all you who are really alive
must have crept from a pile of corpses
executing miracles.

Now all things relative
roar in and out of mind on a motorbike
hugging the black roads.
With strange and mysterious orders
you strangle your love
and let those mechanical fingers
play in the bright transistors
to carry the news to the Mafia.

Shout your hurrahs to the crowd!
In two shakes of anyone's tail
you can hide from the Bomb.
And sometimes you steal through the lust of velvet jackets
into juicy steaks;
and sometimes you press your quick and aching flesh
into tiny yards,
into tight and intimate rooms;

Артемий Михайлов

"Если ты не был в концлагере"

Если ты не был в концлагере,
Если тебя не пытали,
Если твой лучший друг не писал на тебя
        анонимку,
А ты не вылезал из-под кучи трупов,
Чудом уцелев при расстреле,
Если ты не знаешь теории относительности
И тензорного исчисления,
Если ты не можешь мчаться на мотоцикле со
        скоростью в двести километров,
Если ты не убивал любимую, повинуясь чужому
        приказу,
Если ты не умеешь собирать полупроводниковые
        радиоприемники,
Если ты не принадлежал к какой-либо мафии
И не умеешь самозабвенно кричать "ура"
        вместе со всеми,
Если ты не можешь за две секунды спрятаться
        от атомного взрыва,
Если ты не умеешь одеваться за счет питания,
Если ты не можешь жить впятером на пяти
        квадратных метрах
И даже не играешь в баскетбол,
То ты не человек XX века.

and sometimes, like a sport,
you go flinging the bouncing ball
through the iron hoop and the webbed cone
just to be living, just to be really living,
just now.

N. NOR

TO MY FRIENDS

It's not for us to train the trigger
on the heart of the green column.
The poet works with other wishes.
Police and troops are strong.

No hymns for soldiers now are born
in this decisive hour;
we live for the imaged thought alone
though bludgeons crack the town.

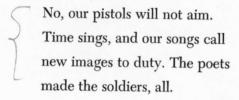No, our pistols will not aim.
Time sings, and our songs call
new images to duty. The poets
made the soldiers, all.

Н. Нор

Моим друзьям

Нет, не нам разряжать пистолеты
В середину зеленых колонн!
Мы для этого слишком поэты,
А противник наш слишком силен.

Нет, не в нас возродится Вандея
В тот гудящий, решительный час!
Мы ведь больше по части идеи,
А дубина - она не для нас.

Нет, не нам поднимать пистолеты!
Но для самых ответственных дат
Создавала эпоха поэтов,
А они создавали солдат.

BULAT OKUDZHAVA

SONG ABOUT STUPID PEOPLE

This is the way in our new age:
for every high tide there's a low tide,
for every clever one a stupid one;
everything's just and e-qual.

Not everyone stupid likes it thus;
they even look stupid far away.
"Stupid, stupid!" the people shout,
and none of them like this very much.

Why should stupidity have to blush,
if we all were given a la-bel
and classified, classified long ago
so everyone knows everybo-dy?

The labels have sold for a long time;
for a dollar you'll get a whole pound now;
the stupid ones seem like the cle-ver,
and the clever ones more like the stu-pid.

This is the way in our new age:
for every high tide there's a low tide,
for every clever one a stupid one;
everything's just and e-qual.

Булат Окуджава

ПЕСЕНКА О ДУРАКАХ

Вот так уж ведется на нашем веку -
на каждый прилив по отливу,
на каждого умного по дураку,
всё поровну, всё справедливо.

Но принцип такой дуракам не с руки, -
с любых расстояний их видно.
И все им кричат: "Дураки! Дураки!"
А это им очень обидно.

И чтоб не краснеть за себя дураку,
чтоб каждый был выделен, каждый,
на каждого умного по ярлыку
повешено было однажды.

Давно в обиходе у нас ярлыки,
по фунту на грошик на медный.
И умным кричат: "Дураки! Дураки!"
А вот дураки незаметны.

BULAT OKUDZHAVA

THREE LOVES, THREE WARS,
THREE DECEITS

First love burns and glows in your heart;
and second love remembers the first.
But the third one . . .

> the key rattles the lock;
> the key rattles the lock,
> your suitcase in hand.

The first war? Oh, it's nobody's fault;
and maybe the second is somebody's fault,
but the third war . . .

> it is my very own fault;
> it is my very own fault,
> as anyone can see.

And the first lie, like a morning mist;
the second one, like a drunken head,
but the third lie . . .

> dark, darker than night,
> dark, darker than night,
> redder than war.

Булат Окуджава

"А как первая любовь - она сердце жжёт"

А как первая любовь - она сердце жжёт,
а вторая любовь - она к первой льнёт,
ну, а третья любовь - ключ дрожит в замке,
ключ дрожит в замке, чемодан в руке.

А как первая война - да ничья вина,
а вторая война - чья-нибудь вина,
а как третья война - лишь моя вина,
а моя вина - она всем видна.

А как первый обман - на заре туман,
в второй обман - закачался пьян,
а как третий обман - он ночи темней,
он ночи темней, он войны страшней.

BULAT OKUDZHAVA

LEN'KA KOROLYOV, THE KING

The evening record player in the yard
made couples dance amidst the dust,
and the boys thought Len'ka Korolyov was a king.
They named him that, in simple trust.

He *was* a king. If any of his friends
had trouble or things went wrong
each knew the royal hand would help him then,
cleverly ringed with steel, and strong.

But one day when the Messerschmitts, like ravens,
dove and ripped his silent door
our king put on his cap, just like a crown
tipped back on his neck, and went to war.

Now the record players in the yards
blare at the sun, but none are seen
weeping for him. You see, it was like this:
he had no chance to court himself a queen.

Wherever I go now, troubled as I am,
working, sneaking, or moping around
corners and the next yards, I dream I'll meet
my earthly sovereign on that ground.

Булат Окуджава

ЛЕНЬКА КОРОЛЕВ

Во дворе, где каждый вечер всё играла радиола,
где пары танцевали, пыля,
ребята уважали очень Леньку Королева
и присвоили ему званье Короля.

Был Король,как король, всемогущ, и если другу
станет худо и вообще не повезет,
он протянет ему свою царственную руку,
свою верную руку и спасет.

Но однажды,когда "мессершмитты", как вороны,
разорвали на рассвете тишину,
наш Король,как король, он кепчонку,как корону,
набекрень, и пошел на войну.

Вновь играет радиола, снова солнце в зените,
да некому оплакать его жизнь.

Потому что тот Король был один - уж извините,
королевой не успел обзавестись.

Но куда бы я ни шел, пусть какая ни забота,
по делам или так, погулять,
все мне чудится, что вот за ближайшим поворотом
Короля повстречаю опять.

Потому что на войне, хоть и, правда, стреляют,
не для Леньки сырая земля,
потому что,виноват, но я Москвы не представляю
без такого, как он, короля.

Because of war, you know, they all shoot straight.
From this damp earth we heard him sing.
I can't imagine that Moscow'll be the same,
without our Len'ka, our own king.

BULAT OKUDZHAVA

THE SONG OF AN AMERICAN SOLDIER

I pick up my uniform, rucksack, and helmet,
and paint it all in camouflaged colors.
Then I march in the winding streets. It's easy
to become a soldier, to become a soldier.

And then I forget my domestic troubles;
I don't have to work, don't have to make money.
I just fool around and play with the rifles.
Oh, it's easy to soldier; it's easy to soldier.

If something goes wrong, that's not our business.
As the saying goes, we serve our country!
It's great not to care at all what I'm doing
and just be a soldier, just be a soldier.

Булат Окуджава

"Возьму шинель и вещмешок и каску"

Возьму шинель и вещмешок и каску,
в защитную окрашенные краску,
ударю шаг по улочкам горбатым -
как просто стать солдатом, солдатом!..

Забуду все домашние заботы,
не нужно ни зарплаты, ни работы.
Иду себе, играю автоматом -
как просто быть солдатом, солдатом!

А если что не так - не наше дело.
Как говорится - "Родина велела!"
Как славно быть ни в чем невиноватым,
совсем простым солдатом, солдатом!

THE SONG OF FRANÇOIS VILLON

As long as planets circle the sun,
or there is light above the grave,
dear Lord God, give to everyone
    all that he doesn't have.
Give intellection to the clever;
to quaking cowards give a horse,
and lots of money to lucky ones.
    Remember me, of course.

As long as planets circle the sun,
whatever is in your power, Lord,
give power to the power-hungry
    to rule until they're bored.
Give generous breaks to generous ones;
and even as a day's remorse
remember Abel, let Cain repent.
    Remember me, of course.

I know you're always powerful,
knowing and merciful and wise;
like any soldier killed, I'll live
    forever in your eyes.
Each listening ear of every man
believes your quiet words; we go
and always trust in what you do
    and not in what we know.

Булат Окуджава

ФРАНСУА ВИЙОН

Пока земля еще вертится, пока еще
                    ярок свет,
Господи, дай же Ты каждому,
                    чего у него нет:
мудрому дай голову, трусливому дай
                    коня,
дай счастливому денег...
                    И не забудь про меня.

Пока земля еще вертится - Господи,
                    Твоя власть! -
дай рвущемуся к власти
                    навластвоваться всласть,
дай передышку щедрому,
хоть до исхода дня,
Каину дай раскаяние...
                    И не забудь про меня.

Я знаю: Ты все умеешь,
                    я верую в мудрость Твою,
как верит солдат убитый, что он
                    проживает в раю,
как верит каждое ухо тихим речам
                    Твоим,
как веруем и мы сами, не ведая,
                    что творим!

O Lord, my awesome green-eyed God,
as long as planets circle the sun—
and even that's hard to believe—
until all time is done,
please give a little for all of us;
also remember me, of course.
Give, please, a bit for all of us,
and remember me, of course.

Господи мой Боже, зеленоглазый
мой!
Пока земля еще вертится, и это ей
странно самой,
пока ей еще хватает времени и огня,
дай же Ты всем понемногу...
И не забудь про меня.

BULAT OKUDZHAVA

WHEN WE LEAVE

When, at last, we have traveled
                    in the desert or under the rain,
our mothers, those first explorers of our souls,
stand at our doors
                    discovering further lands.
And the hearts of the mothers
burn in those thoughts
                    like flames.
O hearts, hearts, and native lands,
is there always someone waiting
in those places where we finally come,
following those mirages that lead us on?
Well, it's all the same when toward this autumn land
                    the great cranes are flying.

Булат Окуджава

"Когда мы уходим"

Когда мы уходим
                    (хоть в дождь, хоть в сушь),
у ворот стоят наши матери -
первооткрыватели наших душ,
как материков
                    открыватели.
А сердца матерей горят кострами.
(Те костры в расставании жгут.)
Ах, сердца, вы сердца - родимые
                                  страны,
где нас непременно ждут,
где мы якоря свои бросили,
и куда б нас чудеса ни завели,
все равно в те страны по осени
улетают
        наши журавли.

YURY PANKRATOV

STORMY NIGHTS

When lightning intersects the skies
and lilac trees whip in the wind,
your cheeks, beloved, wet with rain,
  like enamel shine.

Changing, the birch trees, white as sheets,
hang in that wind. I see you stand:
your white face in the crying lilacs,
  barefoot, with laughing hands.

When lightning darts the evening sky,
lovely women, the legends say,
are born, and freedom lifts the voice,
  and even strong men fail.

When fiery words upbraid the sky
and earth is dark with lilac air,
you and I fly everywhere,
  greedy beyond despair.

But how soon you wither in the mind,
lilacs in shining wrappers. This
is how we touch our lips, how in
  all weathers we will kiss.

Юрий Панкратов

ГРОЗА НОЧЬЮ

Когда по небу ходят молнии,
Деревья кажутся лиловыми,
А щеки милые и мокрые
Становятся эмалированными.

Как будто наволочку в прачечной,
Березу кружит и бросает,
А ты стоишь в сирени плачущей
Смеющаяся и босая!

Когда по небу ходят молнии,
Родятся женщины красивые,
И возникают песни вольные,
И умирают люди сильные.

Когда по небу ходят возгласы,
Земля наполнена духами,
А мы летим с тобой по воздуху
И грудь на полное дыхание.

Но как торопко ты померкла,
Сирень в блестящем целофане.
О, эта робкая примерка
Двух губ при первом целованьи!

FRIEND

Painter, I need a portrait of a friend.
Paint small and childlike shoulders,
easy and slender hands.
And make the fingers long, not Russian;
use the sensitive neck of a girl,
and an Adam's apple, marked by a tie
to give it the likeness of a man,
and a noble jaw.
Then make the whole mouth fleshy,
as large and purpled
as that of a clown,
and the thin nose like a bird's beak.
Let all that hair be helpless as straw,
and the eyes,
let the eyes give back
the horror of all they saw.

Муза Павлова

Художник, нарисуй мне друга"

Художник, нарисуй мне друга,
чтоб были у него мальчишеские плечи,
неторопливые худые руки
и пальцы длинные, нерусские,
и шея недотроги,
кадык, подчеркнутый воротничком,
ему с мужчиной придающий сходство,
и благородный подбородок,
и рот, как намалеванный,
мясистый
преувеличенный и алый, как у клоуна,
и нос надменный, птичий,
и под соломою беспомощных волос
глаза,
в которых
остался ужас перед жизнью.

A. Petrov

THE ROMANTIC HAZE

Oh, the blue haze of the romantics
and the burning heart of Danko,
what floods of blood and water rush
the cellars of the
        Lublyanka.

Oh, the blue haze of the romantics,
in Budapest the tanks, oh,
floods of blood and water rush
the cellars of the
        Lublyanka.

Oh, the blue haze of the romantics
with foot rags for our souls, oh,
floods of blood and water rush
the cellars of the
        Lublyanka.

А. Петров

"Эх, романтика, синий дым"

Эх, романтика, синий дым,
Обгоревшее сердце Данки...
Сколько крови, сколько воды
Утекло в подземелье
                    Лубянки.

Эх, романтика, синий дым...
В Будапеште - советские танки.
Сколько крови, сколько воды
Утекло в подземелье
                    Лубянки.

Эх, романтика, синий дым,
Наши души пошли на портянки.
Сколько крови, сколько воды
Утекло в подземелье
                    Лубянки.

GENRIKH SABGIR

RADIO NIGHTMARE

He sprawls on the bed.
No one's there.
Just the black box on the wall
in which a folk choir is shouting.
He stretches hard and yanks the cord!
He jams it in again.
How can he believe his ears?
Over the noise and crackling metallic sounds
he finally hears
a human voice:
Latest news bulletin,
special edition!
. . . on the place
of the crime . . .
overwhelming majority,
. . . barometric pressure rising . . .
rising danger of nuclear attack.
Epidemic . . .
War . . .
The plans have been overfulfilled!

And then the choir again,
the jet engine singing.
Explosion . . .
Ovation!

Генрих Сабгир

РАДИОБРЕД

Лежа, стонет.
Никого нет.
Лишь на стенке черный рупор,
В нем гремит народный хор.
Дотянулся, дернул шнур!
Штепсель тут, розетка там.
Не верит своим ушам:
Шум,
Треск,
Лязг металла,
Радио забормотало:

"Последние известия,
экстренное сообщение!
... На месте
Преступления.
... Большинством голосов.
... Градусов
Мороза.
... Угроза
Атомного нападения.
Эпидемия...
Война...
Норма перевыполнена!"
Снова хор. На фоне хора
Соло авиамотора,

The sick man sprawls with glassy eyes.
He jerks. He grabs the blanket.
In the door, far, far away,
someone
appears.
Doctor,
let's check the bolts.
Radio: *The Moonlight Sonata*
is being performed on balalaika.

Рев
Реактивной авиации,
Взрыв
Овации!
Больной глядит остеклянело.
Рука
Судорожно сжала
Одеяло.
Из дверей - издалека
Показался некто.
- Доктор!
- Надо
У меня проверить гайки.
Доктор:
"Лунная соната
Исполняется на балалайке".

THE DEATH OF A DESERTER

Are you a deserter?
No, sir, I just lost my unit.
OK. Shoot him on the spot.

Is this, maybe, just a bad dream?
Bushes, precipice, river,
bridge,
clouds in the sky.
A squad of impassive faces.
An officer.
A feather-light twist.
A dive bomber howling.
The bomb.
A mass of glass
smashing the air!

Hit!
Officer, ambulance!
Alive?
Carry him!
His guts
are falling out!

A mosquito, whining and complaining,
circles his forehead.
In his unit he was gloomy,
wasn't he? Worried.

Генрих Сабгир

СМЕРТЬ ДЕЗЕРТИРА

- Дезертир?
- Отстал от части.
- Расстрелять его на месте!
(Растерзать его на части!)
Может быть, все это снится?..
Куст,
Обрыв, река,
Мост
И в солнце облака.
Запрокинутые лица
Конвоиров,
Офицера.
Там воздушный пируэт -
Самолет пикирует,
Бомба массою стекла
Воздух рассекла -
Удар!..
Наклонился конвоир -
Офицер -
Санитар.
- Еще живет?
- Нести?
Разрывается живот.
Вывалились внутренности.
Сознания распалась связь...
Комар заплакал, жалуясь,

The roof of his house leaked.

His pear trees,

unpicked,

rotted.

And the apples,

unsprayed,

were wormy.

His boar pig went scrawny

and dropped in the barn.

There was no wood for the winter.

And his wife? That bitch!

A juicy woman with red lips;

she had a good time, all right.

That's all she cared for.

She'll say, "OK, baby,

they got him on the lost list for good;

he died serving his country,

or, more likely, they court-martialed him

in the line of duty!"

And he took his hammer,

climbed up the roof

and in his anger

and wild longing

he hit the nails

into the boards

hard!

But the nails

got into his belly,

Вьется и на лоб садится,
Не смахнуть его с лица...

По участку ходит мрачен,
Озабочен:
На доме прохудилась крыша,
На корню
Засохла груша,
Черви съели яблоню,
Сдох в сарае боров,
Нет на зиму дров.
А жена? Жена румяна,
На щеках горят румяна.
Она гуляет и поет -
Никого не узнает.
Говорит: "Чудные вести:
Пропал без вести,
Пал героем,
Расстреляли перед строем!"
Взял молоток,
Влез на чердак
И от злости
И тоски
Забивает гвозди
В доски,
Всаживает
В свой живот.
Что ни гвоздь,
То насквозь!

one by one,
oh!
    Oh.

    Hey, watch out!

    He's still alive!

    Well, drop him.

    Where the hell do you want to take him?

    His guts are ripped.

Still,
the mosquito buzzes, buzzes.
"Hey, guys,
spare me!
Don't
kill me!"

Нестерпимая резь.
Ай!
Ой!
- Посмотри, еще живой.
- Оставь, куда его нести,
Вывалились внутренности.
(Комар не отстает, звеня.)
- Братцы, не убейте меня.

PAVEL VLADIMIROV

CHAPELS

Over Russia chapels stand,
　forsaken and forgotten;
over Russia chapels stand,
　glorious for nothing.

Sighs and moans, creaks and groans,
　old women of the wild wood,
all they can remember now
　is time past, and childhood.

Golden cupolas are dulled,
　crosses ripped with violence;
the bells are stilled and rusted now,
　the country filled with silence.

Standing alone upon the steppes
　in villages and roads,
their people have forgotten them,
　forgotten, too, God's words.

They pierce the world with empty eyes,
　impotently demanding
something they have not ever known,
　loyal understanding.

Павел Владимиров

"Стоят церквушки по Руси"

Стоят церквушки по Руси
Забытые, забитые,
Стоят церквушки по Руси
Ничем не знаменитые.

Вздыхают, охают, кряхтят
И как старухи молятся,
О старине былой грустят,
Припоминают молодость.

Не блещут златом купола,
Покошен набок крест,
И не звенят колокола,
Шум наводя окрест.

Стоят одни на пустырях,
В деревне, у дорог,
Забыли люди о церквах,
Забыл о них и Бог.

На мир глядят из темных дыр,
Им непонятен век,
Им непонятен новый мир
и новый человек.

The winds of time have blown away
old men and older nations;
still over Russia the chapels stand,
lost in their own salvations.

ANDREY VOZNESENSKY

SHAME

They have cut out our sense of shame
like an appendix.
We are doomed, shameless.
We are overcoming death, but who knows how
to blush for life?

These are the fibrillose membranes of our cheeks,
the soul's sense of touch,
a gift from God,
not ears and eyes.

When I go down
into the filthy lives of men
shame scorches my cheeks
like a flatiron.

Shame, how we hold our tongues,
or hem and haw.
I am ashamed
of some of my poems.

Lies on fat faces
should lie hidden in trousers.
But what of the shame
when the king of a country
pauses before taking off a shoe

Андрей Вонесенский

СТЫД

Стихи, прочитанные на 200-ом
спектакле "Анти-миров"

(Фрагмент)

Нам как аппендицит
Поудаляли стыд.
Бесстыдство наш удел.
Мы попираем смерть.
Но кто из нас - краснел?

    Сквозь ставни наших щек
    Не просочится свет.
    Но по ночам как шов
    Заноет - спасу нет!

Я думаю, что Бог
Заместо глаз и уш
Нам дал мембраны щек
Как осязанье душ.

    Горит моя беда.
    Два органа стыда
    Не только для бритья,
    Не только - для битья.

Спускаюсь в чей-то быт,
Смутясь, гляжу кругом -

and wonders,
"Which foot
did I wash yesterday?"

And now—it's scandalous—
all the newspapers in Greece
look alike.
Vietnam becomes a pawn.
We lie and lie.

And what if we do eat fish
with a fork instead of a knife,
or eat
while others starve?

Oh, you intelligentsia,
you are caught in the toughening tissue of your lies,
reading Herzen
while stripping, bare-ass, for the lash.

Мне гладит щеки стыд
С изнанки утюгом!

Как стыдно мы молчим,
Как минимум - хохмим.[+]
Мне стыдно писаний
написанных самим.

Ложь в рожищах людей -
Хоть надевай штаны.
Но может быть стыдней
Когда король страны
Мучительно заколебался прежде чем снять
         туфлю на трибуне заседания.

Елки-моталки - размышлял он.
Ведь точно помню - вымыл вчера ногу.
Но - какую? Левую или правую?

                                        еще

Постыдно,
Когда в Греции введена цензура,
И все газеты похожи одна на другую.

Постыдно,
Когда Вьетнамом играют как фишкой
Лгать, лгать постыдно!

Постыдно рыбу брать,
Не вилкой, а ножом.

[+] Разговорное выражение "попытка острить".

Стыдней, что неча жрать
Другим, когда мы жрем.

Сверхклассик и сатрап,
Стыдытесь, дорогой,
Чужой роман содрал -
Не смог содрать второй.

    "Интелигенция",
    Как ты изолгалась.
    Читаешь Герцена,
    Для порки заголясь!

А лучший режиссер
Чернеет с простыней,
Как корчится костер...
Но тыщи раз стыдней,

    Что нам глядит в глаза -
    Как бы чужие мы -
    Хрустальнейшей страны
    Застенчивый укор застенчивых лугов,
    Застенчивая дрожь застенчивейших рощ ...

Обязанность стиха
Быть органом стыда.

AIDA YASKOLKA

VARIATIONS ABOUT MYSELF

It's all the same to me
whose windows I stare at on a winter night,
or on whose hearth I lie, soaking wet,
stretching my hand for the vodka.

I don't care
what I accept and what I don't,
whose souls I blunder in,
or whether I slash my wrists
or pull the noose on someone's neck.

It's all the same to me
whatever law I tremble under
and what meadows I must cross.

But secretly before the icon
I pray, "Do not forget me, God;
forgive me for what I do,
for tears of triumphant lies.
And for myself and others,
give me strength, dear God, to resist
as long as I live."

Аида Ясколка

ВАРИАЦИЯ О СЕБЕ

Мне все равно в какие окна
Я в зимний вечер загляну
На чей огонь зайду промокнув
И руку к рюмке протяну
Кого приму иль оттолкну
Чью душу невзначай задену
Себе ли перережу вену
Другим ли петлю затяну
Мне все равно под чьим законом
Дрожать и по полям каким
Бродить но тайно у иконы
И не оставь и не покинь
Меня Господь прости мне встречи
Неправды слезы торжества
И дай мне сил противоречить
Себе и всем пока жива

ANNA AKHMATOVA

REQUIEM

A Cycle of Poems

No, never! Not in foreign skies,
not safe beneath some other star;
but here with my own, I swung my eyes
there where we were, and where they are.

IN PLACE OF A FOREWORD

In the terrible years of the Yezhovshchina I have spent seven-teen months standing in queues in front of the prisons of Len-ingrad.

Once, someone recognized me.

In that moment, a woman standing behind me—who in all probability had never heard of my name—suddenly came to her senses from the overpowering numbness affecting us all, and with her lips blue from cold whispered into my ears (everybody whis-pered there), "Can you describe this?"

And I answered, "Yes, I can." And something of a smile ap-peared there where her face once was.

Leningrad
April 1, 1957

Анна Ахматова

РЕКВИЕМ

Нет, и не под чуждым небосводом,
И не под защитой чуждых крыл -
Я была тогда с моим народом,
Там, где мой народ, к несчастью, был.

ВМЕСТО ПРЕДИСЛОВИЯ

В страшные годы ежовщины я провела
семнадцать месяцев в тюремных очередях в
Ленинграде. Как-то раз кто-то "опознал"
меня. Тогда стоящая за мной женщина с
голубыми губами, которая, конечно, никог-
да не слыхала моего имени, очнулась от
свойственного нам всем оцепенения и спро-
сила меня на ухо (там все говорили шепо-
том):
- А это вы можете описать?
И я сказала:
- Могу.
Тогда что-то вроде улыбки скользнуло
по тому, что некогда было ее лицом.

1 апреля 1957 года
Ленинград

DEDICATION

Urals would crack and bend in all this grieving,
Volgas freeze and block their misty breath.
Prison locks are strong beyond believing;
under them the convict bunks are heaving,
grayed and set against the hue of death.

Somewhere in the chill of evening falling
people, still enchanted by the sun,
calm themselves. But we, apart, are calling.
Down that rustling silence, so appalling,
Human keys and iron soldiers run.

And we awoke. As if for early praying,
we marched together, each a single ghost,
heard what all the empty streets were saying.
Sunny mists above the Neva playing
sang of hope, that far untraveled coast.

Then a sentence. Someone's tears were breaking
on that vast sea that sentenced her, alone;
pain in every heart there sharply waking
drove her to stumble homeward, bent and shaking,
stalking the heavy pavement like a stone.

Where are you now: friends, strangers, fearing
those two remorseless years and years of hell?

ПОСВЯЩЕНИЕ

Перед этим горем гнутся горы,
Не течет великая река,
Но крепки тюремные затворы,
А за ними "каторжные норы"
И смертельная тоска.
Для кого-то веет ветер свежий,
Для кого-то нежится закат -
Мы не знаем, мы повсюду те же,
Слышим лишь ключей постылый скрежет
Да шаги тяжелые солдат.
Подымались как к обедне ранней,
По столице одичалой шли,
Там встречались, мертвых бездыханней,
Солнце ниже и Нева туманней,
А надежда все поет вдали.
Приговор... И сразу слезы хлынут,
Ото всех уже отделена,
Словно с болью жизнь из сердца вынут,
Словно грубо навзничь опрокинут,
Но идет... Шатается... Одна...
Где теперь невольные подруги
Двух моих осатанелых лет?
Что им чудится в сибирской вьюге,
Что мерещится им в лунном круге?
Им я шлю прощальный свой привет.

Март 1940

What Siberian snowstorm, ever nearing,
wreathes those eyes, a thousand moons appearing?
Now, if I can, to all I send farewell.

March 1940

PROLOGUE

Only the dead, this age, were laughing,
serene, happy, undisciplined.
Leningrad staggered, its own self staffing
prisons like rotting signs in the wind.

This was the age, condemning
grief, half mad, out walking
to the lost farewells, failing
where the whistling trains sang.

The Star of Death had come to try us.
Russia, pure in its roots,
rolled to the wheels of its Black Marias
and writhed under bloodied boots.

1. THEY CAME FOR YOU IN THE MORNING

They came for you in the morning.
And I followed you, dark as a sack.
Deep in their rooms the children were sobbing.
On the icon the candle went black.
On your lips the chill of that statue
broke like a shroud on our dying,
and I go—could I ever forget you?—
like the wives of the Streltsy, crying.

1935

ВСТУПЛЕНИЕ

Это было, когда улыбался
Только мертвый, спокойствию рад.
И ненужным привеском болтался
Возле тюрем своих Ленинград.
И когда, обезумев от муки,
Шли уже осужденных полки,
И короткую песню разлуки
Паровозные пели гудки.
Звезды смерти стояли над нами,
И безвинная корчилась Русь
Под кровавыми сапогами
И под шинами черных марусь.

1. УВОДИЛИ ТЕБЯ НА РАССВЕТЕ

Уводили тебя на рассвете,
За тобой, как на выносе, шла,
В темной горнице плакали дети,
У божницы свеча оплыла.
На губах твих холод иконки.
Смертный пот на челе... Не забыть! -
Буду я, как стрелецкие женки,
Под кремлевскими башнями выть.

1935

2. QUIET FLOWS THE QUIET DON

Quiet flows the quiet Don;
moonlight puts a window on,

throws its cap upon its back,
yellow, sees the shadows crack.

Woman dead, or woman quick,
tell me, is this woman sick?

Husband in the grave, and he,
her son, in prison. Pray for me.

3. NO. NO, IT'S NOT ME

No. No, it's not me. It is someone out there who's crying.
For I know I could not. Let this that happened bury
us with an unutterable darkness.
Let the last candle be taken away. . . .

Night.

2. ТИХО ЛЬЕТСЯ ТИХИЙ ДОН

Тихо льется тихий Дон
Желтый месяц входит в дом,

Входит в шапке набекрень,
Видит желтый месяц тень.

Эта женщина больна,
Эта женщина одна,

Муж в могиле, сын в тюрьме,
Помолитесь обо мне.

3. НЕТ, ЭТО НЕ Я

Нет, это не я, это кто-то другой страдает.
Я бы так не могла, а то, что случилось,
Пусть черные сукна покроют,
И пусть унесут фонари...
            Ночь.

4. WOULD YOU HAVE KNOWN

Would you have known yourself in that halo
if you knew your own means and your ends,
sinning gaily at Tsarskoye Selo,
you mocker and favorite of friends
queueing up here with these three hundred,
each with a parcel under this cross,
to melt the icy year with hunger
and the long cold tears of loss?

In the wind all the poplars are frozen. . . .

We wait, in the silence, outside. . . .

Inside, the innocent, chosen . . .

5. SEVENTEEN MONTHS

Seventeen months I've been crying where
they keep your home. Not here.
At the foot of the executioner
I threw my terror and fear.
How could I sort confusion out?
My grief I do not know.
Who is the brute? How long to wait
for the executioner now?

4. ПОКАЗАТЬ БЫ ТЕБЕ

Показать бы тебе, насмешнице
И любимице всех друзей,
Царскосельской веселой грешнице,
Что случится с жизнью твоей -
Как трехсотая, с передачею,
Под Крестами будешь стоять
И своей слезою горячею
Новогодний лед прожигать.
Там тюремный тополь качается,
И ни звука - а сколько там
Неповинных жизней кончается...

5. СЕМНАДЦАТЬ МЕСЯЦЕВ

Семнадцать месяцев кричу,
Зову тебя домой.
Кидалась в ноги палачу,
Ты сын и ужас мой.
Все перепуталось навек,

И мне не разобрать
Теперь, кто зверь, кто человек,
И долго ль казни ждать.
И только пыльные цветы,
И звон кадильный, и следы
Куда-то в никуда.
И прямо мне в глаза глядит
И скорой гибелью грозит
Огромная звезда.   1939

Church bells and the rustic flowers
Dry their footprints on these hours
   and chain us where we are;
staring into my eyes, I see
peril forever threatening me
   with its enormous star.

1939

6. WEEKS HAVE SO QUICKLY RISEN

Weeks have so quickly risen
that I do not know what's done,
or how the staring nights, my son,
looked down at you in prison.
Living hawks with fiery eyes,
gazing where we turn and toss,
dangle wings on your high cross
and talk a death of lies.

1939

7. THE SENTENCE

And now the word, like a rock, has fallen
into my breast and its living pit.
But it's all the same. I had made it common
and was prepared. I'll get over it.

As for today, why, I can mock
myself just killing thoughts, and then
harden my soul to a solid rock,
learning to live. I'll do it again.

No, that's not it . . . these summery conditions
appeared behind my window to carouse
long, long ago among these premonitions:
this strange bright day, and this all-empty house.

Summer 1939

6. ЛЕГКИЕ ЛЕТЯТ НЕДЕЛИ

Легкие летят недели,
Что случилось, не пойму.
Как тебе, сынок, в тюрьму
Ночи белые глядели,
Как они опять глядят
Ястребиным жарким оком,
О твоем кресте высоком
И о смерти говорят.

1939

7. ПРИГОВОР

И упало каменное слово
На мою еще живую грудь.
Ничего, ведь я была готова,
Справлюсь с этим как-нибудь.

У меня сегодня много дела:
Надо память до конца убить,
Надо, чтоб душа окаменела,
Надо снова научиться жить, -

А не то... Горячий шелест лета,
Словно праздник за моим окном,
Я давно предчувствовала этот
Светлый день и опустелый дом.

1939. Лето

8. TO DEATH

Well, Death, come on at once since you'll come anyhow
    in this hard life. You are my groom,
You, who are strangely great and plain, and coming now,
    I have switched off the light, opened my room.
So come now, Death, and take whatever forms you seek:
    be blasted in your poisonous shell, or
come like a hardened gangster, or like a murderer sneak.
    Infect me like a typhoid dweller.
Or be some fairy tale invented like those views
    familiar unto death . . . such bores!
Or like some secret fellows, brash in ribboned blues,
    parading by cowering janitors.
It's all the same. The Yenisey waves in the sun
    and, over all, Polaris seems
the blue and brilliant eyes of my beloved one,
    hiding from view my harrowing dreams.

August 19, 1939
Fountain House

8. К СМЕРТИ

Ты все равно придешь - зачем же не теперь?
Я жду тебя - мне очень трудно.
Я потушила свет и отворила дверь
Тебе, такой простой и чудной.
Прими для этого какой угодно вид,
Ворвись отравленным снарядом
Иль с гирькой подкрадись, как опытный
        бандит,
Иль отрави тифозным чадом.
Иль сказочкой, придуманной тобой
И всем до тошноты знакомой -
Чтоб я увидела верх шапки голубой
И бледного от страха управдома.
Мне все равно теперь. Клубится Енисей,
Звезда полярная сияет.
И синий блеск возлюбленных очей
Последний ужас застилает.

            19 августа 1939
            Фонтанный Дом

9. THE WINGS OF MADNESS

The shady wings of madness hum
and hover in my soul already.
This wine has fired my senses dumb
and lures me down the darkest valley.

That this will triumph, wrong on wrong,
I understand. I understand.
Though all my nightmares could belong
to someone else, some other hand,

these hands are empty. Nothing here
is kept or left within my care
though you appease the maddened year
and bore me with incessant prayer.

No son with frightened eyes to harm,
no suffering deeply petrified,
nor one day of the broken storm,
nor prison meetings magnified.

Not now the trembling shadow cast
upon his lips, no hand bestirred,
nor loving voices, nor the last
consolation of the word.

May 4, 1940
Fountain House

9. УЖЕ БЕЗУМИЕ КРЫЛОМ

Уже безумие крылом
Души закрыло половину,
И поит огненным вином
И манит в черную долину.

И поняла я, что ему
Должна я уступить победу,
Прислушиваясь к своему
Уже как бы чужому бреду.

И не позволит ничего
Оно мне унести с собою
(Как ни упрашивай его
И как ни докучай мольбою):

Ни сына страшные глаза -
Окаменелое страданье,
Ни день, когда пришла гроза,
Ни час тюремного свиданья,

Ни милую прохладу рук,
Ни лип взволнованные тени,
Ни отдаленный легкий звук -
Слова последних утешений.

4 мая 1940
Фонтанный Дом

10. CRUCIFIXION

"Do not weep for me, mother;
I am flat in my grave."

I

For some the angels praised the holy hour.
The fire of heaven opened on their sleep.
"Oh, why have you forsaken me, my father?"
But to his mother, only, "Do not weep."

II

Magdalene was crying, and the anguished
disciple turned to stone. But where
the mother, in her utter silence, languished
no one even dared to stare.

1940–43

10. РАСПЯТИЕ

"Не рыдай Мене, Мати,
      во гробе сущу"

I

Хор ангелов великий час восславил,
И небеса расплавились в огне.
Отцу сказал: "Почто Меня оставил!"
А Матери: "О, не рыдай Мене..."

II

Магдалина билась и рыдала,
Ученик любимый каменел,
А туда, где молча Мать стояла,
Так никто взглянуть и не посмел.

1940-43

EPILOGUE

I

And there I knew how hollow cheeks belie
the terror shifting in the glancing eye,
and how the runic script of all we suffer
is written on our faces, by and by.
No dark head now, no lovely blond can scorn them,
for they, too, will too suddenly be gray,
and though obedient smiles might still adorn them
fear has its own dry laughter to obey.
Not only for myself I bow, but for
all of us who waited long before
in summer heat and winter cold, and swore
our prayers upon that red-brick wall and door.

ЭПИЛОГ

I

Узнала я, как опадают лица,
Как из-под век выглядывает страх,
Как клинописи жесткие страницы
Страдание выводит на щеках,
Как локоны из пепельных и черных
Серебряными делаются вдруг,
Улыбка вянет на губах покорных,
И в сухоньком смешке дрожит испуг.
И я молюсь не о себе одной,
А обо всех, кто там стоял со мною,
И в лютый холод, и в июльский зной,
Под красною ослепшею стеною.

II

And now, in atoning hours, I can hear
and see, once again, and touch what you were.

You whom we brought to the window for light,
and you who have fallen down earth into night.

And you who said, with your beautiful face,
"I am here, as if I came home," in this place.

And I want to call all of your names who came on
and stood with me here, but your names are gone.

Now that I never will see them again
I have woven a web of their words, for them:

for all that I felt, for all that I heard,
I remember you always. This is my word.

If my tortured mouth should be shut with their lies,
and a hundred million people's cries,

let this still stay, let this song go out
that a hundred million people can shout.

And let them remember, when I am dead,
that if ever this country hears what I said

and someone should say, let us put up a stone,
then let them. But on one condition alone:

II

Опять поминальный приблизился час.
Я вижу, я слышу, я чувствую вас:

И ту, что едва до окна довели,
И ту, что родимой не топчет земли,

И ту, что красивой тряхнув головой,
Сказала: "Сюда прихожу, как домой".

Хотелось бы всех поименно назвать,
Да отняли список, и негде узнать.

Для них соткала я широкий покров
Из бедных, у них же подслушанных слов.

О них вспоминаю всегда и везде,
О них не забуду и в новой беде,

И если зажмут мой измученный рот,
Которым кричит стомильонный народ,

Пусть так же они поминают меня
В канун моего поминального дня.

А если когда-нибудь в этой стране
Воздвигнуть задумают памятник мне,

Согласье на это даю торжество,
Но только с условьем - не ставить его

it must never be set by the side of the sea
where I was born. No, let that be

untouched forever, and as well, those waves
of clean green shadow over the graves

of Tsarskoye Selo. Those gardens are gone
with another I loved, strolling over its lawn.

But here! Where we stood, and stand, and wait,
here at the locked and immutable gate,

because I fear, even when I am rotten
that those Black Marias might be forgotten,

that the slamming iron of heavy doors
will fade in the cannon of all our wars,

and that those women, so bravely tall,
will fail like a wounded animal.

So let our tears, like melted snow,
wear down these stones before we go,

and let the prison doves be free
as long as the Neva flows to the sea.

March 1940

Ни около моря, где я родилась:
Последняя с морем разорвана связь,

Ни в царском саду у заветного пня,
Где тень безутешная ищет меня,

А здесь, где стояла я триста часов
И где для меня не открыли засов.

Затем, что и в смерти блаженной боюсь
Забыть громыхание черных марусь,

Забыть, как постылая хлопала дверь
И выла старуха, как раненный зверь.

И пусть с неподвижных и бронзовых век
Как слезы струится подтаявший снег,

И голубь тюремный пусть гулит вдали,
И тихо идут по Неве корабли.

1940. Март

Notes

Because of the nature of underground literature, biographical and other data concerning the poets presented in this volume were not always available. Sometimes we could identify only the sources of the poems for further possible reference.

T. A.
L. T.

page 20   Anonymous: *Etáp*

Grani, Frankfurt am Main, 1965, No. 57, pp. 3–4.

The editors of *Grani* reported: "The poem has been sent to us from Russia. Neither the fate nor the name of the poet is known to us."

Etáp: Russian, from the French *étape*, meaning "way station" or "day's march." The word became Russianized in the nineteenth century in connection with the Siberian exile system. Prisoners were driven from the European part of Russia to Siberia, usually on foot, and the word *etáp* described both the daily stretch they had to march (about twenty miles) and the way station where they were fed and spent the night. The fourth volume of the Soviet dictionary *Tolkovy Slovar'*, published in 1940, defines the word *etáp* as "a method of transporting prisoners by the police authorities in tsarist Russia" (p. 1436). Ironically, Stalin's Russia used not only the word *etáp* but also the nineteenth-century methods of exile. V. I. Jakobi painted a famous picture in 1861 showing a column of prisoners marching in *etáp* to Siberia: *Prival Arrestantov* (A Stopover for the Prisoners). See *Istoriya Russkogo Isskustva*, Moscow, 1960, Vol. II, p. 29.

page 24   Anonymous: *Concentration Camp Song*

Mikhaylo Mikhaylov, *Leto Moskovskoye*, Izd. Possev Frankfurt am Main, 1968, p. 60.

The English version of Mikhaylov's book (*Moscow Summer*, Noonday Press, 1965) only refers to this song; but the Russian edition, from which we took it, carries the complete song. It describes the transport of prisoners by boat from the Vladivostok area to the most dreaded and cursed concentration camp complex, in the Kolyma region of Siberia, in the Arctic Circle. In order to avoid bad international publicity, the boats were disguised by the Soviet authorities as cargo vehicles. These proved to be death ships, as other writers have also testified; see General A. V. Gorbatov, *Years Off My Life,* Norton, 1965, and Eugenia Ginzburg, *Journey into the Whirlwind,* Harcourt, Brace and World, 1967.

page 28   ANONYMOUS: *Dubrovlag*

   Possev, Frankfurt am Main, 1969, No. 3, p. 42.

   This prison song has been quoted by Anatoly Marchenko in *Moi Pokazaniya* (My Testimony), which describes the prison camps of the Brezhnev-Kosygin era. The references to the rebels of the nineteenth century indicate clearly that present-day prisoners of the Soviet regime consider themselves their spiritual heirs. The poem was written in 1966.

page 30   BELLA AKHMADULINA (b. 1934): *Conjuration*

   Bella Akhmadulina, *Oznob* (Shivering), Izd. Possev, Frankfurt am Main, 1968, p. 194.

   The melancholy sadness, the feeling of "paradise lost," of predestined unhappiness in love because of the lesser quality of the man in love with her, characterize this poem as well as much of Akhmadulina's poetry. They are certainly strange qualities for a "socialist" poet, and they are given even more emphasis by the traditional "Russian" images that dominate the poem: the icon painter, the limping cripple at the church, Petersburg, the literary capital of pre-1917 Russia—all evoking a chain of associations connected with such names as Akhmatova and Tsvetayeva, the women poets of the early twentieth century, to whom Akhmadulina owes much in her poetry. Petersburg, since Pushkin's exile in 1820 connected with the "traditional" contrast between south and north, also evokes a train of literary associations identifying Akhmadulina as an heir to the "Petersburg" tradition of classical Russian literature. The reference to the good-natured beggar (*katorshanka*) going to his jail suggests another famous *katorshanka*, from nineteenth-century Russian literature: Katerina Maslova in Tolstoy's *Resurrection.*

page 32   BELLA AKHMADULINA: *I Swear*

   Ibid., pp. 194–96.

   The poem is dedicated to Marina Tsvetayeva, and apparently refers to one of the last snapshots taken of her in exile in Yelabuga, in Soviet Asia, where she committed suicide in 1943. The African referred to is Pushkin, whose contemporaries used the term because his great-grandfather was an Abyssinian. Pushkin, the poet of fairy tales, such as *Russlan and Ludmilla* (1820), is shown further on in Akhmadulina's poem as a poetic predecessor; his Baba Yaga (the witch of the Russian fairy tales) turns into Yelabuga in modern times. Yelabuga thus not only becomes a mystical beast against whom Akhmadulina carries on her fight, but is also a symbol of Stalinism.

The reference to Tversky Boulevard again connects the poem with the Pushkin period, as well as with the pre-1917 Petersburg where Marina Tsvetayeva lived. The final lines indicate that Akhmadulina considers herself the heir to Tsvetayeva, not just in her poetry but possibly even in her tragic fate.

The nervous quality of the poem is created in the Russian by the constant repetition of the formula "I swear." Russian grammatical construction is such that the verb actually may be omitted. This makes the poem even more exalted, since it likens it to a prayer which, because of constant repetition, becomes so familiar to the worshipers that they omit certain parts of the text, as, for example, the constantly repeated sentence in the Russian orthodox service: *Gospodi pomiluy* (Forgive us, Lord). (See Simon Karlinsky, *Marina Cvetaeva: Her Life and Art,* University of California Press, 1966.)

page 38 BELLA AKHMADULINA: *Bartholomew Night*
        Ibid. pp. 187–89.

A more direct political statement, this poem laments the fate of Akhmadulina's generation, brought up in the atmosphere of the terror of the Stalinist "Bartholomew Nights."

page 44 PAVEL ANTAKOLSKY (b. 1896): *The Stalin Prize*
        Grani, 1964, No. 56, p. 182.

The poem is a good example of the guilt complex of a generation which, voluntarily or not, tolerated or supported the Stalin regime. The feeling could be compared to the "repentant nobleman's" sentiments in nineteenth-century Russian literature, or to the guilt suffered by Germans after the collapse of the Hitler regime (*die unbewältigte Vergangenheit*). The poem was written in 1956.

page 46 ALEXANDER ARONOV: *A Little Geography*
        Grani, 1965, No. 58, pp. 100–1. Originally in *Sintaxis,* No. 1, 1959.
        Original title: "Verses About Countries."

page 50 VLADIMIR BATSHEV (b. 1946) *Voices*
        Grani, 1966, No. 61, pp. 12–13.
        Original title: "To Karelan."

Vladimir Batshev, born in Moscow, is said to be the son of a high-ranking official in the office of state censorship. His work has appeared in underground literature since 1964. In the summer of 1965, at the "illegal" poetry reading at the Mayakovsky Square in Moscow, Batshev recited several poems by Pasternak. His own poems were "published" in the following underground periodicals: *Masterskaya* (Workshop), *Chu, Sfinxy, Sheya* (Neck). He has also published short stories in SMOG collections, and two individual volumes of poetry: *Labirint* (Labyrinth) and *Sinny Korabl'* (Blue Ship).

Batshev participated in the demonstration of April 14, 1965, demanding artistic and personal freedom for political prisoners such as Naritsa, Bukovsky, Ossipov, and Brodsky. Batshev and some of the others were arrested by the KGB and beaten. After his release he took part in demonstrations demanding freedom for Sinyavsky and Daniel. Batshev was arrested once more on December 2, 1965, and sent to the Matrosskaya Tishina psychiatric hospital in Moscow, which is one of the main prisons for political dissenters. After his release, Batshev joined the committee preparing a demonstration on the forthcoming anniversary of Stalin's death (March 5, 1953), aimed at protesting "re-Stalinization" in the Soviet Union. He was arrested again on February 24, 1966, and sent this time to the Lefortovo prison. Denied an open trial, he was sentenced for "parasitism" and sent to a concentration camp in the summer of 1966. (*Grani*, 1966, No. 61, pp. 3–4.)

The date set under this poem is the anniversary of Stalin's death.

page 52   VLADIMIR BATSHEV: *Now the State Needs Me*
           Grani, No. 61, p. 13.

page 54   VLADIMIR BATSHEV: *Sonnet to Pasternak*
           Grani, No. 61, p. 6.

Batshev obviously considers Pasternak one of the most important poets of Russia, and speaks of him with reverence and the humble attitude of a pupil (". . . for I am small"). The poem refers to much that dominates the Russian poetical heritage of the twentieth century which the Soviet regime has destroyed; the connection of Russian poetry with the West (bridges) is symbolized also by the names of the two cities, Petersburg and Marburg, where Pasternak had been a student in 1913. Petersburg is emblematic of cultural ties with Europe; the references to the classical Greek culture (the four Muses) are a reminder that Pasternak practiced three of the arts: music, poetry, painting. Symbols used in Pasternak's poetry resound in Batshev's sonnet: e.g., May, spring, as life-giving and supporting elements. The Litfond (*Literaturny Fond*) is a subsidiary organization of the Writers' Union for the support of needy writers; this was the only official Soviet organization which dared to mention Pasternak's death openly. The Writers' Union ignored it.

page 56   VLADIMIR BATSHEV: *Sonnet to L. K.*

Grani, No. 61, p. 5.

page 58   VLADIMIR BATSHEV: *Variations on a Theme of Joseph Brodsky*

Grani, No. 61, pp. 6–8.

This is one of the "Decembrist" poems of Batshev, in which he draws a parallel between his fate and that of the famous rebels of the Russian nineteenth century: the Decembrists and the Narodovoltsy (the People's Freedom movement of the second half of the century). V. Bukovsky is a member of the Soviet underground arrested in 1965. The "poems wailed by a tomcat" refers to the prologue of Pushkin's *Russlan and Ludmilla*.

page 62   VLADIMIR BATSHEV: *Sonnet to G—ov*

Grani, No. 61, pp. 8–9.

G—ov is probably Yury Galanskov, a leader of the Soviet underground, poet ("The Human Manifesto"), and literary critic and editor of the underground periodical *Phoenix 1966*. He was serving a seven-year sentence in a prison camp when he died in 1972.

The references to December are possibly twofold: December 1825, the Decembrist uprising, and December 1965, when the underground organized a demonstration demanding the liberation of Sinyavsky and Daniel (arrested in September 1965 and then awaiting their trial, in February 1966). The "Commander" may signify both the commanding officer of the 1825 uprising and Galanskov, the "commander" of the new "Decembrists."

page 66   VLADIMIR BATSHEV: *Pushkin at the Senate Square*

Grani, No. 61, pp. 10–12.

Another "Decembrist" poem, loaded with allusions to the 1825 uprising and parallels to the state of the Soviet underground. The Senate Square in Petersburg was the site of the uprising on December 14, 1825. The "rebellious carré" was led by young officers. Pushkin was not in Petersburg at that time, since he lived in exile at his estate in Mikhaylovskoye: therefore he could not participate in the uprising, although he sympathized with the rebels. However, when Nicholas I asked him in 1826, "What would you have done if you had been in Petersburg on the fourteenth of December?" Pushkin answered, "I should have been in the ranks of the rebels." (E. J. Simmons, *Pushkin,* Harvard University Press, 1937, p. 253.) Here Batshev identifies himself with Pushkin, who, though not of his own volition, missed the uprising at the Senate Square. Batshev and his poetic hero missed it, too, in a double sense: in 1825, and for the second time in 1965. Natalya is Pushkin's wife, but the poetic Natalya is probably the hero's fiancée. Ryleyev is one of the young poets, a friend of Pushkin's, who was hanged after the failure of the uprising. The other participants were sent to Siberia to mine lead. Pushkin wrote a poem of greeting to them. In the last part of his poem Batshev recalls the end of the uprising: the rebellious soldiers were surrounded and shot by loyal troops.

The final reference to the Senate Square, identifying it with the Mayakovsky Square in Moscow, is the most pregnant expression we have of a feeling of identity between the Decembrists of 1825 and the present-day Soviet dissidents. The Mayakovsky Square in Moscow was the place for "illegal" poetry readings in the early sixties, and here practically all of the Soviet dissenters began their careers. The identification of the two movements lends this poem a tragic note, since the outcome of the Decembrist uprising is well known.

page 72 VLADIMIR BATSHEV: *Yelabuga*

Grani, 1969, No. 70, p. 114. Originally in *Chu* (collection of SMOG poems).

Batshev's poem, dedicated to Marina Tsvetayeva, radiates the atmosphere of the old Russian holy places—as represented on the icons—where great saints, holy men, and *yurodivye* (God's fools) lived withdrawn from the world. The colors, the "jam" (*varenye*), the monasteries, all remind the reader of the stylized beauty of the medieval Russian religious world, and probably indicate that Yelabuga, a place of horror for Tsvetayeva, was her Golgotha, which in the Christian tradition became holy and transfigured through a sacrifice. The white monks, the dancers (angels), and the iconlike primitivism create an atmosphere of "the sky-blue monasteries"—heaven.

page 74 DMITRY BOBYSHEV: *Upon the Launching of a Sputnik*
Grani, No. 58, p. 163. Originally in *Sintaxis,* No. 3, 1960.

page 78 DMITRY BOBYSHEV: *A House Was There*
Grani, No. 58, p. 166. Originally in *Sintaxis,* No. 3.

Bobyshev's poem is a good example of the unheroic approach to the theme of the Second World War, which in official literature is treated only in pathetic terms.

page 82   VLADIMIR BURICH: *Confessions of a City Dweller*
Grani, No. 58, p. 102. Originally in *Sintaxis*, No. 1.

page 84   SERGEY CHUDAKOV: *Drowning*
Grani, No. 58, p. 131. Originally in *Sintaxis*, No. 1.

page 86   YURY TIMOFEYEVICH GALANSKOV (1939–1972): *The Human Manifesto*
Grani, No. 52, pp. 46–48, originally in *Phoenix I.*

The poem was written in 1961. It contains allusions to Marx and Engels' *Communist Manifesto*. Galanskov died in prison in Siberia in 1972, allegedly for gross neglect of his physical health. He was arrested for the first time in 1961 for distributing the underground periodical *Phoenix* and spent several months in a "psychiatric" hospital. He was arrested again on January 19, 1967, for distributing *Phoenix II*, 1966, for which he was tried in 1968 together with Ginzburg, Dobrovolsky, and Lashkova, and was sentenced to seven years of hard labor.

page 96   ALEXANDER GALICH: *Ballad of the Blue Bird*
Grani, No. 70, pp. 113–14.

Galich is a poet-bard, who usually performs his song poems accompanying himself on the guitar. This song deals with a typical Galich topic: the fate of the former *zeks*, who find it difficult to come to terms with the lost years of their lives spent in the concentration camps of the Stalin era. Here Galich is recounting the entire history of the Soviet prison camp system, the different layers of the camp population. The first ones who were arrested and sent to the camps were punished for the "banner of blue"—they were the idealists, fighting for the blue bird of world revolution. Ironically, however, blue has a different symbolic meaning as well: it is the color of the epaulets and caps of the NKVD soldiers. Thus the color blue becomes an ambiguous symbol, indicating both the idealists and the NKVD, who arrested the idealists, supposedly also for idealistic reasons. On the basis of paragraph 58 of the Criminal Code, fifteen years' imprisonment was the standard sentence for "anti-Soviet political activity." The *zeks* died not like soldiers, but as numbers, since their names were obliterated in the camps (as Solzhenitsyn describes it in his *One Day in the Life of Ivan Denisovich*).

The geographical names give a check list of the most infamous death camps of the Stalin era. The second layer of the camp population consisted mainly of Communist Party members who were sent to the camps during the "Great Purges" of the thirties. They were punished for the red banner.

During the Second World War the *zeks* who were "reliable" were sent to the front in punitive battalions where they were subjected to the yellow color of exploding mines and grenades. The *zeks* were usually used as cheap and expendable minesweepers; they were driven through the minefields to clear the way for the regular troops, who were following, and were killed—"blinded" by the white of the explosions, which reflected the eyes of the dying *zeks*, also turning white. The former *zek* cannot be certain of the reasons for his past suffering, since searching for causes and the people responsible for the camps is once again taboo in the Brezhnev-Kosygin era. The song ends with a typical Galich picture: the former *zek* sitting in a pub, drinking, is unable to tear himself away from his memories and become assimilated into "normal" Soviet life.

page 100 ALEXANDER GALICH: *Conjuration*

Grani, No. 68, pp. 7–8.

This is again a song poem, telling the story of a retired NKVD officer (possibly even Khrushchev himself, who had a luxurious dacha at the Black Sea) who has achieved the highest dream of a Soviet civil servant: the personal pension, a greater amount of money than is provided by the state pension plan. The personal pension is the surest sign of the Soviet VIP. Allowing himself liberties, which he formerly would not, the officer visits a popular restaurant to mingle with the "simple people." But it turns out that the pleasures of the "folk," as well as the entire *nekul'turno* (uncivilized) atmosphere of the public beach at the Black Sea (he is used to the cultivated atmosphere of the more exclusive NKVD resorts), annoy him. He also realizes that he is alone, and cannot associate with ordinary people. Taking a walk at the seashore, he finds that even the Black Sea is against him. In his dream he is in service again, and sends the Black Sea by *etáp* to Inta (one of the concentration camps in Siberia) for *kontra*, or counterrevolutionary activity. The Vokhrovtsy (Russian abbreviation for *Voyenisirovannaya Okhrana*—Military Type Camp Security Forces), the equivalent of the SS in German concentration camps, are the men most hated by the *zeks*. (See, for example, Solzhenitsyn's *The Cancer Ward* and Aksyonov's *Halfway to the Moon*.)

"Forgive us our sins" is taken from the prayer of the ortho-dox service, corresponding to the *Miserere Nobis* of the Roman Catholic Mass. The blasphemy of the NKVD man, and the cleaning woman lighting a candle for the deceased NKVD officer, contrast the values of the communist functionary and those of the ordinary Russian people.

The closing line of the song, "forgive us our sins," empha-sizes once again a trend in Galich's poetry which is also observable in Okudzhava's songs: namely, that only a return to religious values can redeem and solve the hopeless contradictions of post-Stalinist Soviet society.

page 106 ALEXANDER GALICH: *Clouds*

    Grani, 1965, No. 59, p. 24. Originally in *Sfinxy*, No. 1, 1965.

Here again, the former *zek*, half drunk, watches the clouds fly to Abakan (another concentration camp in Siberia), just as mem-ories of his life, destroyed in the camps, drift across the screen of his memory.

page 110 ALEXANDER GALICH: *Silence Is Golden*

    Grani, No. 59, pp. 26–27. Originally in *Sfinxy*, No. 1.

Galich's song deals with one of the essential aspects of the national guilt complex for the crimes of the Stalin era: the silence and tolerance of violence by the great majority of the people.

page 114 GLEB GARBOVSKY: *After the War*

    Grani, No. 58, p. 172. Originally in *Sintaxis*, No. 3.

The "underground" quality of the poem is shown by its "dispassionate" nonpartylike treatment of the topic. Instead of accusing "the imperialists" of warmongering, as would befit a good Soviet patriot, Garbovsky merely points to the possible consequences of an all-out atomic war in which neither political system can survive.

page 118 GLEB GARBOVSKY: *Telephone Booth*

    Grani, No. 58, p. 173. Originally in *Sintaxis*, No. 3.

The poem definitely lacks "socialist realist" qualities: it does not radiate optimism, but rather feelings of *vanitas vanitatum* and *memento mori*.

page 120 GLEB GARBOVSKY: *To the Neva*

    Grani, No. 58, p. 171. Originally in *Sintaxis*, No. 3.

    Obviously a *zek* poem.

page 122 YEVGENY GOLOVIN: *Song of Old Party Members*
      Grani, No. 59, p. 28. Originally in *Sfinxy*, No. 1 (1965).

      This poem refers to the limits of "liberalization" after Stalin's death. It attacks the cynicism of the tactical moves of the party from the point of view of an old Bolshevik. Instead of accepting the official party arguments about the "cult of personality," he accuses the entire regime of bloodshed.

page 124 SERGEY KALASHNIKOV: *Wife*
      Grani, No. 58, p. 147. Originally in *Sintaxis*, No. 2, 1960.

page 126 SERGEY KALASHNIKOV: *Spring in the Office*
      Grani, No. 58, p. 145.

page 130 IGOR KHOMIN: *Idyll*
      Grani, No. 58, pp. 126–27. Originally in *Sintaxis*, No. 1.

page 134 VLADIMIR KOVSHIN: *Now That I Know*
      Grani, No. 59, p. 39. Originally in *Sfinxy*, No. 1 (1965).

page 136 YEVGENY KUSHEV: *The Decembrists*
      Grani, 1967. No. 66, pp. 26–34. Originally in *Russkoye Slovo*, July 1966.

      This is an important "Decembrist" poem, following the poetic pattern of the idol of the Ryleyev Club (which was responsible for the publication of the underground periodical *Russkoye Slovo*), Kondraty Fyodorovitch Ryleyev, the poet-revolutionary who inspired the 1825 uprising. Kushev's cycle of ten poems is dedicated to the memory of the executed leaders of the revolt, and raises the question of similarities between their position and that of present-day rebels in the Soviet Union. All were hanged on July 13, 1826. Among them were:

M. Bestuzhev (1803–26), a republican and leader of the Southern Society.

P. G. Kakhovsky (1797–1826), an advocate of resolute actions, such as seizing the Winter Palace and arresting the czar and his family.

S. I. Muravyev-Apostol (1796–1826), cofounder of the secret society Union of Salvation and leader of the uprising in the province of Chernigov.

K. F. Ryleyev (1795–1826), whose patriotic poems, romantic in style, expressed his deep concern with the course of Russia's history and Russia's place among the civilized nations of the world.

P. M. Pestel (1793–1826), army officer, one of the founders of the Southern Society and author of the revolutionary program of this society, *Russkaya Pravda* (Russian Truth).

The "precise parade" is a reference to the main hobby of Nicholas I (czar from 1825 to 1855), the suppressor of the Decembrist uprising, who liked military parades to be executed with the precision of marionettes.

"The Exiled" refers to the several thousand people involved in the uprising who were exiled to Siberia. The survivors were allowed to return to European Russia only after Nicholas I's death.

Pechorin was the hero of Y. Lermontov's novel *A Hero of Our Times* (1840), a representative of the Byronic alienated hero of the period.

page 148 Artyemy Mikhailov: *Song About Crooks*

Grani, No. 59, p. 47. Originally in *Sfinxy*, No. 1.

Mikhailov's rage is directed at the "new class" (in Djilas' phrase) of the supposedly classless Soviet society.

page 152 Artyemy Mikhailov: *Conditions*

Grani, No. 59, p. 47. Originally in *Sfinxy*, No. 1.

page 156 N. Nor: *To My Friends*

Po Sovietskomu Soyuzu (KRS), New York, April 12, 1968. Originally in *Phoenix 1961*.

The poem is a refutation of the terroristic tradition of the Russian revolutionary movement. The bludgeon refers to an old pre-1917 revolutionary song that calls for violence.

page 158 Bulat Okudzhava (b. 1924): *Song About Stupid People*

Grani, No. 56, p. 186.

The ironic and playful division of people into clever and stupid ones may be understood as an ironic reference to the division of the population of the Soviet Union into two categories: party members and non-party members. The first are by definition always right, while the second category has to toe the line. Okudzhava is *the* poet-bard of the Soviet Union; his poems and songs are very popular all over the country. In a rare public statement after a concert he had given in 1967 in Poland, Okudzhava revealed the following about his poetry and himself:

"I am not a guitar player or a pop ballad singer. My compositions have little in common with popular music concerts.

They are verses which I perform to guitar accompaniment. The music molds and retains memories. It seems to me that such music creates the right kind of mood for singing these song poems. Professional musicians have tried to compose music for my verses and to make orchestral arrangements of my modest melodies. So far, however, their attempts have not been successful. To me, personally, the words and the intonation are more important than the music. I may be going way back to the beginnings of the musical (bardic) form of poetry. That may be so. But assuming that it is, this is not deliberate or conscious on my part. My one ironbound rule is not to have any plans or projects regarding my work. I write when I am moved to do so, under the influence of the most diverse, and frequently not specifically defined, stimuli or moods. For instance, I have not written any verses in the past three years. Now, for example, though impressions and whole stanzas keep going around in my head, I can't say definitely when I shall write a song about Poland. It may be in a few days, a few years, or never. I can afford to be completely spontaneous as far as the small poetry-music forms are concerned. At present I am writing a solid historical novel where I make use of the research and archives studied at the time I was working on a play about the Decembrists, which was written for young audiences. I have the fictional plot and the ideology all mapped out. The principal characters are Pavel Pestel, one of the real leaders of the conspiracy, and the fictional character of an impoverished noble from a remote provincial locality who became the secretary of the czar's Investigating Commission. The plot will focus on problems of the relationship between the state and the individual. I shall try to enclose in this book my experience of contemporary man. The form is based on the great tradition of nineteenth-century Russian prose. I owe most to Dostoyevsky, to his psychological insights and genius in delineating character.

"I began to write verse, like everybody else, in my childhood. While still a young boy, I volunteered to fight in the World War and was wounded several times. After the war, I finished at the University of Moscow. For the next six years, I taught in a small village school in the Kaluga region. There, for lack of competition, I was acclaimed as the first poet of the region. When I moved to Moscow, I discovered at last how bad my verses really were although they had been published and praised. That was a powerful and very beneficial blow. In a year, I began to write differently. At about that time, I also began to sing my songs to guitar accompaniment. At first, I only did this (for a few years) in the circle of my immediate friends. In 1960, I made my first public appearance.

"I don't think I have any attitude toward my own work or that I can say anything about it. As I said, I never promise or plan anything ahead. As regards form, I adhere to tradition. Although I understand and respect unrhymed and unrhythmical poetry, it nevertheless seems to me alien, amorphous, and impoverished in what I feel is its essential feature. That is why I served an apprenticeship to and still study the classics and those contemporary writers who remain loyal to tradition. First among these are Villon, Pushkin, Kipling (his poems), and Boris Pasternak. I also place Juliam Tuwim among the writers I hold dear. It might be that other Polish poets are more highly valued than Tuwim. But although I myself have translated Rozewicz and Grochowiak (with the help of a literal translation) I have remained loyal to Tuwim. Reading some of his poems, I have the feeling that if he had not written them I would have had to do it. Tuwim took life in the same way I do—with sadness and irony. That reaction is perhaps quite general among poets, that is, people who are thin-skinned, who are more acutely aware of the imperfections of the world. For that reason, I have always felt that there is something dubious in one-hundred-percent seriousness. And one-hundred-percent gaiety makes me panic.

"Irony and sadness, that is my maturity as a writer: I owe it, in a decisive degree, to the war. It is not surprising that the war recurs so often in my verses and that it is the subject of my autobiography, my first prose work, published in Poland under the title *Jescze Pozyjesz* [You'll Live a While Yet], and of the two scenarios which have been made into films. In the war I became aware of my own weaknesses; I learned that although a great deal depends on human effort and will, yet man is dependent on objective circumstances, for which he often pays with his suffering, happiness, and even life. In the war I became angry at the cruel fate which had unjustly taken so many of my friends and relations. But at the same time, I learned the great art of forgiveness and understanding. The war taught me not to admire parades or to take the splendid playing of the military band too seriously, though I like it in comedy or operetta. To me war has not yet ended, for I still see its victims. War, which rescues politicians from their predicaments, destroys the humanly necessary stability and is a threat to the bonds between the present and the past—ties which are a condition for further evolution.

"Since I tried to express the above self-evident truth in my creative work, I was called pacifist. That is not quite correct. If someone were to threaten my home, I would take up a stick. If an enemy attacked my country, I would shoot, though without jubilant exaltation. I believe that young soldiers should not be taught to hate their potential or hypothetical enemy. They should be told about love and flowers so that they will want to defend the world they love.

"Love is the subject of many of my song poems. For a long time we heard no songs about love and the word "woman" seemed indecent. In protest against deception and puritanical hypocrisy I was the first who dared, after so many years, to sing in Russian about the inviolability of woman and to fall to my knees before her. I confess that I could never be ironical in this respect. If I have laughed, I have only laughed at myself, as the hero of songs which spoke of the fumbling and bungling male.

"I would like to see love occupy the place it deserves in human life. I would not wish human society to be turned into an army camp; I would like to see all relics of the personality cult vanish from the face of my earth and democratic custom become established as a universal habit. I would like man to feel that he is a fully responsible architect of life. That is why the great nineteenth-century Russian writers who stand up for man and his freedom are so dear to me." [*Poland*, illustrated magazine, published in Warsaw, December 1967, p. 7.]

page 160 BULAT OKUDZHAVA: *Three Loves, Three Wars, Three Deceits*

Bulat Okudzhava, *Proza i Poeziya*, Izd. Possev, Frankfurt am Main, 1968, p. 154.

Okudzhava performed this song in Paris in 1967, when he was allowed to appear before a foreign audience. Its particular beauty derives largely from the strange discrepancy that exists between the music and the content—the music imitating the traditional Russian Gypsy songs, while the content of the text is anything but traditional.

page 162 BULAT OKUDZHAVA: *Len'ka Korolyov, the King*

Proza i Poeziya, p. 131.

This is one of the best-known early antiwar songs that Okudzhava wrote in the style of the "new war literature" of the post-Stalin era, placing man and not military victories in the focus of attention.

page 166 BULAT OKUDZHAVA: *The Song of an American Soldier*

Grani, No. 56, p. 187.

A very popular antimilitary song by Okudzhava. Originally he used to announce it only as "Song of a Soldier." Upon protest by the Soviet Communist Party he added the adjective "American."

page 168 BULAT OKUDZHAVA: *The Song of François Villon*

Proza i Poeziya, p. 221.

First performed in Paris in 1967, this poem shows a new development in both philosophy and music. A religious turn marks the content, and is underlined by the elements of church music and Okudzhava's serious performance.

page 172 BULAT OKUDZHAVA: *When We Leave*

Proza i Poeziya, p. 161.

page 174 YURY PANKRATOV: *Stormy Nights*

Grani, No. 58, p. 112. Originally in *Sintaxis*, No. 1.

page 176 MUZA PAVLOVA: *Friend*

Grani, No. 58, p. 112. Originally in *Sintaxis*, No. 2.

page 178 A. PETROV: *The Romantic Haze*

Po Sovietskomu Soyuzu (KRS), New York, April 12, 1968, p. 6. Originally in *Phoenix 1961*.

Petrov forcefully contrasts the romantic promise of the revolution (the blue haze of romantics) with its unexpected results: Lublyanka, the prison made famous during the tortures of the Great Purges; and the imperialist spirit of Soviet Russia exemplified by Soviet tanks oppressing the Hungarian uprising of 1956.

Danko was a lengendary romantic revolutionary, whose tragic story was told by Gorky in his romantic tale, *Mother Izergil* (1894).

page 180 GENRIKH SABGIR: *Radio Nightmare*

Grani, No. 58, pp. 120–21. Originally in *Sintaxis*, No. 1.

page 184 GENRIKH SABGIR: *The Death of a Deserter*

Grani, No. 58, pp. 119–20. Originally in *Sintaxis*, No. 1.

The underground nature of the poem is shown not only by the nonheroic treatment of an unheroic aspect of the war, but also by the oblique references to the activity of the Soviet Secret Military Police, called also SMERSH (*Smert' Spionam*—Death to Spies), during the Second World War.

page 190 PAVEL VLADIMIROV: *Chapels*

Grani, No. 59, p. 23. Originally in *Sfinxy*, No. 1.

page 194 ANDREY VOZNESENSKY (b. 1933): *Shame*

Po Sovyetskomu Soyuzu (KRS), New York, September 8, 1967, p. 3.

This poem was written by Voznesensky as a reply to the decision of the Soviet authorities not to let him travel to the United States in June 1967. Voznesensky was the only Soviet poet invited to recite his poetry by the organizers of the New York Lincoln Center Summer Festival in 1967. The Soviet authorities at first agreed to the invitation; but they withdrew permission to travel a few days before the opening of the festival and informed Western newspapermen that Voznesensky was sick and could not attend. However, they "forgot" to inform Voznesensky that he was "sick," and the poet found out from Western reporters that he was not going to the festival for "reasons of health." In his fury about the humiliating circumstances of this game, Voznesensky wrote this poem and read it to an audience at the Moscow Taganka Theater. Simultaneously he sent a letter of protest to the editors of *Pravda* (Truth) with a request to publish the "truth" in this matter. *Pravda*, of course, has never published it. But the letter eventually reached the West and was published here in *The New York Times* of August 11, 1967.

Alexander Herzen (1812–70), Russian writer and news-paperman, was editor of the famous émigrée periodical *Kolokol* (Bell). Voznesensky's reference to Herzen is interesting—once again a comparison with nineteenth-century revolutionary traditions, which Voznesensky, as well as the majority of the Soviet underground, considers vastly superior to the present-day cowardice of the Soviet "intelligentsia." The "king of a country" is a reference to Khrushchev, who at a session of the United Nations took off his shoe and banged the bench with it to express his disagreement. The Soviet press never reported the incident, but it became widely known anyway, and contributed to the general aversion to Khrushchev's *"nekul'turno"* (uncivilized) behavior.

page 200 AIDA YASKOLKA: *Variations About Myself*

Grani, 1967, No. 64, p. 112. Originally in *Phoenix 1966*.

page 202 ANNA AKHMATOVA (1889–1966): *Requiem*

Anna Akhmatova, *Sochineniya I*, Inter-Language Literary Associates, 1965, pp. 353–62.

First complete text published in 1963 as a single volume by *Tovarishchestvo zarubezhunykh pisateley* (Association of Writers Living Abroad), Munich, Germany; also in *Grani*, No. 56, pp. 11–19. Although certain parts of the text have already been published in the

Soviet Union, publication of the whole text has never been allowed. Part 7, "The Sentence," appeared in the Soviet literary periodical *Zvezda*, 1940, No. 3–4, p. 75, without a title; it was also included in the 1961 collection of Akhmatova's poetry under the title "1934." The first four lines of Part 9, "The Wings of Madness," were quoted in *Zvezda*, 1946, No. 9, p. 194, in I. Sergievsky's article, *Ob anti-narodnoy poezii Akhmatovoy* (On the Anti-People Poetry of Akhmatova), which was part of the political attack on Akhmatova after the Second World War, led by the Leningrad party secretary, A. Zhdanov. The *Izbranniye Stikhi* (Selected Poetry), 1943, carries the poem under the title "To a Friend," but omits the fourth stanza completely.

The complete rehabilitation of Akhmatova, and the publication of her *Requiem*, was one of the major demands of the liberal Soviet critics during the so-called de-Stalinization years. Actually it was Andrey Sinyavsky himself who voiced such a demand in his congratulatory article on the occasion of Anna Akhmatova's seventy-fifth birthday in May 1965 (*Novy Mir*, 1965, No. 6, pp. 174–75). Sinyavsky quotes here, without mentioning the source, the first dedicatory stanza of the *Requiem*. In "legal" Soviet publications the *Requiem* is mentioned and described in very vague terms, but never quoted. See, for example, A. I. Pavlovsky's biography, *Anna Akhmatova* (*Ocherk Tvorchestva*), Lenizdat, 1966.

"Yezhovshchina" (Foreword): the reign of terror between 1936 and 1938 in the Soviet Union, connected with the name of the Chief of the Secret Police, N. I. Yezhov (1884–1939?), who was killed, presumably in 1939, by his successor in office, Beria.

"Black Marias" (Prologue): Covered trucks used for transporting prisoners. Solzhenitsyn observes in his novel *The First Circle* (1969, abroad), that in the 1950s the Black Marias were camouflaged as transport vehicles carrying "meat" or other merchandise.

"Wives of the Streltsy" (1): The *streltsy* (riflemen) were the secret police of Peter the Great. In 1698 the *streltsy* took advantage of Peter's absence from Russia (he was traveling in Western Europe) and staged a rebellion, which was put down. Returning from abroad Peter took bloody revenge and executed the *streltsy* publicly at the walls of the Kremlin. The wives and female relatives of the *streltsy* sent a delegation to Peter and tried futilely to persuade him to spare the lives of their husbands and children. The nineteenth-century Russian painter, V. I. Surikov, has painted a grandiose picture of the scene: "On the morning of the *strelets* execution" (1884). See *Isstoriya Russkogo Isskustva*, Moscow, 1960, Vol. II, p. 64.

Akhmatova's reference to this bloody tradition of Russian history indicates her understanding of Stalin's cruelties as the continuation of an awful feature of the Russian national fate.

. . . *empty house* (*opustely dom*): according to the evidence of Lidiya Chukovskaya, this poem, written in the summer of 1939, must have been known among at least some of the Russian intellectuals the very same year. Chukovskaya herself selected these very words as the title of her account of the terrible year 1938–39, written at the end of 1939 and the beginning of 1940. See L. Chukovskaya, *The Deserted House*, Pan Books, London 1967.

Blue ribboned: reference to the blue epaulets and caps of the secret police, NKVD.

Janitors: The arresting NKVD officials usually picked up the janitor first in order to find the room or apartment of the person to be arrested more easily. Because of the unbelievably poor housing conditions, even single rooms were shared by several people or families, and it was the janitor's duty to know the location of everyone in the building.

Yenisey, Polaris: Akhmatova refers to the most hated and feared concentration camp complex in the Soviet Union, in the Kolyma region.

Do not weep . . . In the original this is written in Old Church Slavonic, the language of the Russian Orthodox Church.

window: Akhmatova is referring to the window-like opening of the Office of Information at the Leningrad prisons, where the women tried to secure some information about the whereabouts of their arrested husbands or sons. This was necessary because the police did not tell the relatives of the arrested anything about the prisoners. Even at the Information Window, the information received amounted only to the confirmation or denial that the person looked for was detained at the particular prison. Since there were a number of prisons in Leningrad, the task of finding out the whereabouts of a prisoner was usually very time-consuming. Akhmatova mentions seventeen months in "In Place of a Foreword."

"your names are gone": The women lining up in front of the "window" often compiled a sort of check list of the names of those present so that they could notify one another in case they heard anything about someone else's relatives. Since the police wanted to obscure the identity and number of those arrested, such lists were usually confiscated if the police found out about them.

"stone": the lines dealing with the thought that a monument could be erected to her are obviously fashioned after the ideas of Pushkin's poem "Exegi monumentum . . ." Both Akhmatova's and Pushkin's final wills include their evaluation of the place their poetry has in the history of the Russian nation. Both cherish the same idea: to have been the poet of freedom and the mouthpiece of suffering.

"Tsarskoye Selo," "shadow": Tsarskoye Selo is the old name

for the city of Pushkin, where the czars built their summer palaces. The cities of Petersburg and Pushkin were the lifeblood of Akhmatova's poetry, both in the nineteenth-century tradition and in her appreciation for the poetry of the twentieth century.

About the Editors

Joseph Langland was born in Minnesota and is a graduate of the University of Iowa. He has been a teacher ever since, with time out for army service during the Second World War, and since 1959 has been on the faculty of the University of Massachusetts in Amherst, where he is a professor of English. He is the author of several volumes of poetry, including *The Green Town* and *The Wheel of Summer*.

Tamas Aczel was born in Budapest and educated at the University of Budapest. After the Second World War he held various editorial and teaching posts and was deeply involved in the prerevolutionary movement of writers and intellectuals. During the revolution of 1956 he worked as Premier Imre Nagy's press secretary, and escaped from Hungary in November of that year. He is now on the English faculty of the University of Massachusetts in Amherst and is the author of numerous books.

Laszlo Tikos was born in Hungary and studied at the universities of Debrecen and Budapest. He left his native land because of his part in the uprising of 1956 and took his doctorate in Slavic and East European Studies at the University of Tübingen in 1962. Since 1962 he has been teaching Russian language and literature at the University of Massachusetts in Amherst. He has published many articles and reviews and has edited two books.

73 74 75 76 77 10 9 8 7 6 5 4 3 2 1